CANADA'S FIGHTING SHIPS

Historical Publication 12.
Canadian War Museum, National Museum of Man,
National Museums of Canada
John Swettenham, Editor

*Publications in this series by the Canadian War Museum, National Museum of Man, may be obtained from:
Marketing Services Division, National Museums of Canada, Ottawa, Ontario.*

(1) Canada and the First World War, by John Swetten-ham, Canadian War Museum, Ottawa, 1968, Bilingual.

(2) D-Day, by John Swettenham, Canadian War Museum, Ottawa, 1969. Bilingual.

(3) Canada and the First World War, by John Swet-tenham. Based on the Fiftieth Anniversary Armistice Display at the Canadian War Museum, Ryerson, Toronto, 1969. Illustrated. Republished in paperback by McGraw-Hill Ryerson, 1973.

(4) Canadian Military Aircraft, by J.A. Griffin. Queen's Printer, Ottawa, 1969. Bilingual.

(5) The Last War Drum: the North West Rebellion of 1885, by Desmond Morton. Hakkert, Toronto, 1972.

(6) The Evening of Chivalry, by John Swettenham. National Museums of Canada, Ottawa, 1972. Edition française, Le crépuscule de la chevalerie.

(7) Valiant Men: Canada's Victoria Cross and George Cross Winners, edited by John Swettenham. Hakkert, Toronto, 1973.

(8) Canada Invaded 1775-1776, by George F.G. Stanley. Hakkert, Toronto, 1973.

(9) The Canadian General, Sir William Otter, by Desmond Morton. Hakkert, Toronto, 1974.

(10) Silent Witnesses, by John Swettenham and Her-bert F. Wood (*Témoins Silencieux,* adapté par Jacques Gouin). Hakkert, Toronto, 1974.

(11) Broadcast From the Front, Canadian Radio Overseas in The Second World War, by A.E. Powley. Hakkert, Toronto, 1975.

(12) Canada's Fighting Ships, by K.R. Macpherson. Samuel Stevens, Hakkert & Co., Toronto, 1975.

(13) Canada's Nursing Sisters, by G.W.L. Nicholson. Samuel Stevens, Hakkert & Co., Toronto 1975.

CANADA'S FIGHTING SHIPS

K.R. Macpherson

Samuel Stevens,
Hakkert & Company
Toronto 1975

PHOTO CREDITS: Apart from the exceptions listed below, all photographs reproduced in this book are from negatives held in the Public Archives of Canada.

Pages 9 and 25	Commercial Photo Service, Halifax
Pages 31, 53 and 57	Imperial War Museum
Pages 37, 44 and 59	Author's photos
Page 71	De Havilland Aircraft of Canada, Ltd.
Page 79	Watson Studio, Midland

This book has been written and published with the aid of funds provided by the National Museum of Man, National Museums of Canada. In the writing of this book the inferences drawn and the opinions expressed are those of the author himself, and the National Museums of Canada are in no way responsible for his presentation of the facts as stated.

Research for this book was facilitated by a grant made by the Ontario Arts Council.

Design by Helmut Rath

International Standard Book Number: 0-88866-566-0

Published by A.M. Hakkert Ltd., 554 Spadina Crescent, Toronto, Canada M5S 2J9

This book was set in Helvetica by Attic Typesetting.

Printed and bound in Canada by The Hunter Rose Co.

PREFACE

This book is in no way intended to be a history of the Royal Canadian Navy. That has been accomplished in Dr. G.N. Tucker's *The Naval Service of Canada* and Joseph Schull's *The Far Distant Ships,* from both of which works much of my tabular material has been taken. I have wished merely to set down in affectionate retrospect the principal units and classes of fighting ships that have made up the Royal Canadian Navy during its sixty-five-year history.

Of regrettable necessity, an arbitrary line has had to be drawn between fighting ships and auxiliary craft. No disrespect is intended the latter, a variegated and fascinating group which, it is hoped, may someday be the subject of a second volume. They include in their ranks auxiliary patrol craft, gate vessels, landing craft and repair ships, to mention but a few.

I acknowledge with gratitude the assistance of Dr. W.A.B. Douglas, head of the Directorate of History, NDHQ, and his staff; John Burgess; Lt. Cdr. J.K. Steele; Capt. (N.) C. Cotaras; Fred Gaffen, of the Canadian War Museum; and Peter Robertson, of the Public Archives of Canada.

Canada's Fighting Ships is dedicated to John Harbron, my good friend of thirty-five years and the original source of my interest in ships.

KRM

CONTENTS

Introduction / Page 3
Cruisers / Page 5
Armed Merchant Cruisers / Page 12
Aircraft Carriers / Page 16
Destroyers / Page 24
Corvettes / Page 48
Anti-submarine Trawlers / Page 54
Frigates / Page 56
Armed Yachts / Page 62
Destroyer Escorts / Page 64
Hydrofoil Craft / Page 70
Minesweepers / Page 72
Submarines / Page 80
Motor Craft / Page 88
Arctic Patrol Vessel / Page 92
Operational Support Ships / Page 94
Appendix / Page 97

CANADA'S FIGHTING SHIPS

INTRODUCTION

After Britain's conquest of New France, the Royal Navy assumed responsibility for the naval defence of the North American colonies. This eventually made necessary the creation of a freshwater arm of the navy, for during the American Revolution and the War of 1812 the enemy was the United States, and naval engagements were fought on the Great Lakes, the St. Lawrence River and Lake Champlain. By 1776 this obscure British force was known, unofficially at least, as the Provincial Marine. Previously a monopolistic water transport service run by the Admiralty, it had gradually come under the control of the quartermaster-general's department of the army. In 1813, the Royal Navy took over the ships, shore establishments and personnel of the Provincial Marine. By the terms of the Rush-Bagot Convention of 1817, naval vessels were all but abolished from the Great Lakes. The British force on the lakes was, however, revived briefly in the wake of William Lyon Mackenzie's rebellion of 1837-1838, and again during and after the Fenian disturbances of 1866-1870.

In 1867, when the Dominion of Canada came into being, the creation of a navy was not among the new nation's priorities, and the Royal Navy continued to bear the burden of its seaward defence. Prior to 1865 its only Canadian base had been at Halifax, but in that year Esquimalt was formally established for the convenience of the Pacific Squadron, units of which had been using the harbour since 1849. The British naval presence was undoubtedly a major factor in securing British Columbia as a Crown colony until 1871, when it joined Confederation on the strength of a promised transcontinental railway.

That a seagoing country of Canada's stature might be expected to provide for its own naval defence was first suggested by the Admiralty in 1878. The following year it was proposed by the officer commanding the Canadian militia that a naval reserve be formed, and in 1880 the Admiralty offered H.M.S. *Charybdis*, an elderly corvette, as a training ship. She arrived at Saint John in 1881 but soon proved hopelessly decrepit, and the Admiralty agreed to take her back. Although never commissioned as a Canadian ship, *Charybdis* was the first warship owned by the Canadian government. She was sold at Halifax in 1884.

The first decisive step in the direction of a Canadian navy was taken as a result of a naval arms race between Britain and Germany — a race which, in 1909, Britain seemed in danger of losing. That March, the Canadian House of Commons passed a resolution approving the creation of a naval service, a proposal which led to prolonged dissention in the House, the press and the streets. The chief point at issue was whether Canada should contribute money or ships to Britain, or acquire warships of her own. Some favoured neither alternative, but the Naval Service Bill was at last passed on April 20, 1910, and the Naval Service Act received Royal assent on May 4.

Arrangements were promptly made to purchase two old cruisers from the Royal Navy, to serve as training ships. It would have taken an exceptionally gifted prophet to see in them the nucleus of a navy of nearly 500 ships and over 100,000 personnel — the third largest of the Allied fleets.

H.M.S. CHARYBDIS

CRUISERS

The first ship commissioned in the Royal Canadian Navy was H.M.C.S. *Rainbow,* one of two British cruisers purchased in 1910. She had been launched as a "second class protected cruiser" in 1891. She arrived at Esquimalt, which was to be her base, on November 7, 1910, and two days later the base itself was transferred to Canadian control.

Rainbow did virtually nothing until the First World War, when she found herself the Dominion's sole defence against Admiral Graf Spee's squadron of two armoured and three light cruisers. Throughout August 1914, *Rainbow* maintained a search, fortunately fruitless, for the *Leipzig,* which rumour reported everywhere at once. Spee's squadron was defeated in the Battle of the Falkland Islands, December 8, and thereafter *Rainbow* patrolled the Pacific coast as far south as Panama, fairly effectively discouraging German merchant shipping from using coastal waters. In the spring of 1916 she made prizes of two ships considered as engaged on enemy business. She also carried Russian bullion between Esquimalt and Vancouver, to a total of some $140,000,000. In 1917 her crew was more urgently needed in Halifax, and she became a depot ship at Esquimalt until sold for scrap three years later.

The cruiser *Niobe,* larger and better armed than *Rainbow,* had been launched in 1897. She arrived at Halifax on October 21, 1910. The following summer she struck a rock ledge off Cape Sable and was only narrowly saved from sinking. Repairs took until December 1912, and from then until the war *Niobe* spent her time as a stationary training ship at Halifax. Her most important task during the war was contraband patrol off New York as a member of the Royal Navy's 4th Cruiser Squadron. By the summer of 1915 she was largely worn out, and that fall became a depot ship. *Niobe's* upperworks were wrecked in the catastrophic explosion of December 6, 1917, when a munition ship blew up in Halifax harbour,

but she continued in her role until 1920 when, like *Rainbow*, she was sold for breaking up.

RAINBOW at Esquimalt.

NIOBE at Halifax. She was considerably damaged by the explosion of December 6, 1917, and the two funnels she has in the photograh were not hers originally.

A far more modern cruiser, H.M.S. *Aurora*, was presented to the Canadian navy by the Admiralty in 1920, along with two destroyers. Completed in 1914, *Aurora* had seen considerable action in the war, including that off the Dogger Bank in 1915, and she had watched the surrender of the German High Seas Fleet in November of 1918. Post-war cutbacks had, however, doomed her almost from the time of her arrival at Halifax. She was laid up in 1922 and sold for scrap five years later.

AURORA at Halifax.

Two cruisers were transferred from the Royal Navy in the Second World War. One was to have been the 8,800-ton *Superb*, but owing to delay in completion a similar ship of older class, *Uganda*, was substituted. The other was H.M.S. *Minotaur*, a sister ship of *Superb*.

Completed in 1942, *Uganda* had been badly damaged by a glider bomb while supporting Allied landings at Salerno, Italy, in September 1943. She had spent the succeeding year under repairs at Charleston, South Carolina. Commissioned as a Canadian ship in October 1944, she sailed via the Mediterranean Sea to join the British Pacific Fleet. In April 1945 *Uganda* joined Task Force 57 in the Okinawa area, and was thereafter principally employed in screening

ONTARIO, *May 29, 1945.*

10

the Fleet's aircraft carriers as they carried out strikes against Japanese airfields in the Ryuku Islands. On June 14 she led the Fleet in a bombardment of Truk, and a month later was present at the launching of heavy air strikes against Tokyo itself. She left the Fleet late in July, arriving at Esquimalt on August 10, five days before the end of the Pacific war. She was renamed *Quebec* in 1952.

Minotaur, renamed *Ontario*, commissioned in April 1945, too late to see war service. She and *Uganda* spent the remainder of their careers as training ships, one on each coast. *Quebec* was paid off in 1956 and *Ontario* two years later, and both were broken up at Osaka, Japan, in 1961.

QUEBEC, *at high speed off the west coast.*

ARMED MERCHANT CRUISERS

In 1940, when German surface raiders were a more immediate threat than the U-boat, the Canadian government purchased three ships for conversion to armed merchant cruisers. Named *Prince David, Prince Henry* and *Prince Robert,* they were miniature liners of 5,579 tons, completed in 1930 at Birkenhead, England, for Canadian National Steamships.

The conversion of *Prince Robert* was finished in the summer of 1940, but the other two were not ready until the end of the year. Their appearance was radically altered in the process, the top two decks being removed, as well as one of the three funnels, and a cruiser-style superstructure and bridge fitted. Each received four 6-inch and two 3-inch guns, dating from before the First World War. Unlike other armed merchant cruisers of the period, they actually looked like warships and, like many a civilian, seemed decidedly more handsome in uniform.

Prince Robert began her naval career with the capture of the *Weser,* a German freighter acting as supply ship to a raider, off Mexico in September 1940. Late in 1941 she was escort to the transport carrying the ill-fated Canadian garrison to Hong Kong. *Prince Henry* also intercepted two German freighters off Peru, but they were scuttled on her approach and could not be salvaged. *Prince David* meanwhile was serving as a convoy escort on the east coast of Canada.

In May 1942, all three were ordered to the west coast in response to the threat from Japan. After the Japanese occupation of the Aleutian Islands they spent two months on patrol in that area, afterward returning to their duties off the coast of British Columbia. As the changed nature of the sea war had made them ineffective, the three were now on the eve of a second transformation. For *Prince David* and *Prince Henry* this meant conversion to infantry landing ships, while *Prince*

PRINCE ROBERT in 1940, newly rebuilt as an armed merchant cruiser.

PRINCE ROBERT on June 7, 1943, after recommissioning as an auxiliary anti-aircraft cruiser. Twin 4-inch guns have replaced the ancient 6-inch armament she carried as an A.M.C.

Robert was to become an auxiliary anti-aircraft cruiser.

Prince Robert reappeared in her new guise in June 1943, now sporting five twin 4-inch guns, eight 2-pounder pompoms and twelve Oerlikons. For the succeeding year she served as anti-aircraft escort to United Kingdom-Mediterranean convoys, then went home for a refit. Not long after its completion the Pacific war ended, and she was one of the ships that brought released prisoners

home from Hong Kong. She was sold in 1946, and saw sixteen years of merchant service before being broken up.

Prince David and *Prince Henry,* as rebuilt, were fitted to carry eight landing craft, their heavy armament replaced by two twin 4-inch mounts and ten lighter anti-aircraft weapons. Recommissioned at the end of 1943, they went to Clydebank for installation of electronic equipment they would need in the coming invasion of Normandy.

PRINCE HENRY at Taranto, Italy, in March 1945. Originally an A.M.C. like PRINCE ROBERT, she and PRINCE DAVID were converted as landing craft carriers in 1943.

After landing Canadian troops on D Day and afterward, the two were dispatched to the Mediterranean for similar duties in Operation Dragoon, the invasion of southern France. Following this, in the fall of 1944, both took part in the liberation of Greece, with *Prince David* carrying Andreas Papandreou and the members of his provisional government.

At the beginning of 1945, *Prince David* returned to Esquimalt for refit as prelude to her intended use in operations off Southeast Asia. Though transferred to the Royal Navy for this purpose, she was not actually taken over. She was sold to mercantile interests along with *Prince Robert* in 1946, but sailed only five years before being sold for scrap. *Prince Henry* went to the Royal Navy and served for a time as accommodation ship at Wilhelmshaven. Later taken over by the British Ministry of Transport and renamed *Empire Parkeston,* she remained in service until 1961.

AIRCRAFT CARRIERS

The Royal Canadian Navy did not possess any aircraft carriers until after the Second World War, but during the war provided crews for two British carriers, to serve in the Battle of the Atlantic.

A major tactical problem in the Battle of the Atlantic was the mid-ocean gap that lay outside the range of Allied air patrols. An early but far from satisfactory measure was the "CAM" ship — a merchant ship with a catapult on its forecastle from which a Hurricane fighter could be launched. It was primarily designed to counter German Condor bombers — long-range convoy raiders — and a particular drawback was that the fighter, once catapulted off, was almost invariably lost. The pilot's only options were to reach land or to ditch and hope for rescue.

In September 1941 a vastly improved countermeasure, H.M.S. *Audacity,* appeared on the scene. A merchant ship converted into a small aircraft carrier, she was the former German *Hannover,* captured off San Domingo in February 1940. *Audacity* carried six Martlet fighters and, most important, could recover them. She enjoyed a brief but successful career before being torpedoed and sunk that December.

Audacity was the forerunner of 38 "Woolworth" carriers on merchant hulls built for the Royal Navy in American shipyards. Short of manpower by the fall of 1943, the Admiralty proposed that Canada supply crews for two of these little carriers, *Nabob* and *Puncher.* H.M.S. *Nabob,* the first to enter service, embarked the Royal Navy's 852 Squadron of Avengers at San Francisco in February 1944, and March found her at sea with a deckload of Mustang fighters. In August, after several months' training, *Nabob* was in Norwegian waters on an aerial mining operation, and shortly afterward she was part of a force whose object was to attack the battleship *Tirpitz* in her Kaa Fjord lair. On August 22, as the force withdrew, *Nabob* was hit by a torpedo from

U 354, but succeeded in making Rosyth under her own power. She was not repaired for naval service, but reverted to her intended function as a merchant ship after the war.

NABOB aground in the Strait of Georgia during work-ups, January 24-28, 1944.

PUNCHER from the air, May 12, 1944. The flight deck was less than 500 feet long!

H.M.S. *Puncher,* near-sister to *Nabob,* commissioned at Seattle in February 1944, and that July left Norfolk, Virginia with a cargo of forty U.S. Army aircraft for Casablanca. She then returned to Norfolk to take aboard the Corsairs of the Fleet Air Arm's 1845 Squadron, as well as an assorted deckload of American aircraft. After some months exercising, she left Scapa in February 1945 to take part in a strike against German shipping in Norwegian coastal waters. She engaged in two similar operations before the war ended, then entered on a period of service as a troopship. In January 1946 she was handed back to the U.S. Navy at Norfolk, Virginia, and a few years later was converted for merchant service.

Negotiations for the transfer of a light fleet carrier had begun as early as July 1944, but it was not until January 1945 that *Warrior* and *Magnificent* were offered. Both had been launched in 1944, but *Warrior* did not commission until January 24, 1946 and *Magnificent* was to wait considerably longer. *Warrior* embarked the Seafires and Fireflies of 803 and 825 Squadrons and steamed into Halifax at the end of March. Unsuited for an eastern Canadian winter, she was transferred to Esquimalt in November.

It now appeared, however, that the Canadian Navy would be permitted to man only one carrier,

owing to reductions in defence spending, and it was decided to replace *Warrior* with *Magnificent*. In the course of her return to Halifax in February 1947 she called at Havana with destroyers *Nootka* and *Micmac,* the first Canadian warships to do so since 1929. *Warrior* spent most of that year at sea training and, latterly, in preparations for paying off. At the end of 1947 she embarked stores for her successor and in February arrived at Belfast where these were transferred. On March 23, 1948 she was commissioned in the Royal Navy, with which she served until 1958, when she was sold to Argentina and renamed *Independencia*.

Magnificent commissioned on April 7, 1948, more than three years after her launching at Belfast. During the ensuing nine years she was to be unceasingly engaged in training cruises and exercises, sometimes with other Canadian ships, sometimes with British, American and other NATO units. She would visit such scattered ports as Oslo, Lisbon, Havana and San Francisco, and take part in large-scale NATO manoeuvres like "Mainbrace" and "Mariner" in 1952 and 1953.

On December 29, 1956 she sailed from Halifax for Port Said, carrying a deckload of 233 vehicles as

Resembling a sea-going parking lot, MAGNIFICENT *en route to Egypt at the time of the Suez Crisis, in January 1957.*

well as 406 army personnel and stores —
Canada's contribution to the UN Emergency
Force in the Middle East. "Maggie" sailed from
Halifax for the last time on April 10, 1957, to be
turned over to the Royal Navy at Plymouth the
following month. She arrived at Faslane for
breaking up in July 1965, having been laid up in
the interim.

When the Suez crisis erupted *Magnificent* had
just completed landing stores for her successor,
the government having decided to "trade her in"
on a more modern carrier whose construction had
been suspended in 1946. The sleeping beauty's
name was to have been *Powerful,* but Naval
Headquarters renamed her *Bonaventure* for the
bird sanctuary in the Gulf of St. Lawrence. It is
not recorded whether whimsy played a part in the
selection of the name. She had been launched in
February 1946, but work stopped after three

*BONAVENTURE from overhead, her angled deck plainly
visible.*

BONAVENTURE, *with Tracker anti-submarine aircraft and helicopters on deck.*

months, so that later, unforeseen improvements could be built into her. Most notable of these was the angled flight deck, which provided a longer landing run without sacrifice of parking space forward, and permitted removal of the unpopular crash barrier. Also noteworthy were the steam catapult and mirror landing sight — the latter going far toward eliminating human error in landing.

"Bonnie" commissioned on January 17, 1957 and arrived at Halifax on June 26, carrying on deck an

experimental hydrofoil craft built in Britain for the Naval Research Establishment. Unlike her predecessors, *Bonaventure* had Banshee jet fighters and Tracker anti-submarine planes as her aircraft complement. Like them, she enjoyed a busy career of flying training and participation in anti-submarine and tactical exercises with ships of other nations. Her mid-life refit, carried out 1966-67, took sixteen months and cost over $11,000,000. As a result, she became a national *cause célèbre* when she was sold for scrap three years later.

DESTROYERS

The two destroyers received from Britain after the First World War were the *Patriot* and the *Patrician* — modern, three-funnelled craft that had entered service with the Royal Navy in the summer of 1916. Together with the cruiser *Aurora* they commissioned at Devonport in November 1920, and a month later arrived at Halifax. In 1922 the cruiser and two submarines were sold as an economy measure, and the Royal Canadian Navy assumed in embryo the form it was to take until 1940 — a destroyer navy.

Patriot and *Patrician,* worn out by 1927, became stationary drillships on the east and west coasts, respectively. Replacements were ordered in Britain, but pending their delivery the Admiralty agreed to lend Canada two destroyers launched just after the war. These ships, *Torbay* and *Toreador,* were renamed *Champlain* and *Vancouver* and commissioned at Portsmouth at the beginning of March 1928.

In 1929 the contract for the new destroyers was awarded to Thornycroft's, who had built Canada's previous four. They were essentially copies of the Royal Navy's Acasta class, with modifications to suit them for winter operation in the northwest Atlantic. Launched in 1930 as H.M.C.S. *Saguenay* and *Skeena,* and commissioned at Portsmouth the following spring, they arrived at Halifax on July 3, 1931.

Champlain and *Vancouver,* whose loan seems to have become permanent, were discarded in 1936. Arrangements had been completed the previous year for the purchase of the Crusader class destroyers *Crescent* and *Cygnet* from the Royal Navy. Renamed *Fraser* and *St. Laurent,* they were commissioned in February 1937. Two further members of the same class, *Comet* and *Crusader,* were acquired in 1938, commissioning that June as H.M.C.S. *Restigouche* and *Ottawa.* The acquisition of these four ships reflected the

PATRIOT *at Halifax.*

government's concern over the deteriorating international situation.

So it was that Canada entered the war on September 10, 1939, with a fighting force of six destroyers, augmented a few weeks later by the recommissioning of H.M.S. *Kempenfelt* as H.M.C.S. *Assiniboine.* She had been the flotilla leader of the Crusader class, half of which was now in the Royal Canadian Navy and known

CHAMPLAIN.

FRASER in the Panama Canal, probably in April 1937.

collectively as the River class. Otherwise virtually identical to her sisters, *Assiniboine* was fitted with extra accommodation for a flotilla commander and his staff. These seven destroyers were to bear almost the full burden of Canada's growing part in the Battle of the Atlantic until the first corvettes appeared on the scene late in 1940.

In May 1940, with France overrun by the Germans and the invasion of Britain a likely prospect, *Fraser, Restigouche, St. Laurent* and *Skeena* were urgently summoned there. All but *Skeena* took part in the evacuation of troops from the Biscay and Channel ports, and while thus engaged *Fraser* was run down and sunk by H.M.S. *Calcutta.* As the invasion threat diminished, the three remaining returned to North Atlantic convoy duty. One of *St. Laurent's* more memorable achievements was the rescue of some 860 survivors of the British liner *Arandora Star,* sunk July 2, 1940 by a U-boat. Those rescued were Axis prisoners of war, mostly Italian.

H.M.S. *Diana,* acquired in place of the lost *Fraser,* commissioned on September 6, 1940 as H.M.C.S. *Margaree.* She sailed from Londonderry on October 20 and two days later was sunk in collision with a British freighter. Most of *Fraser's* survivors were lost with her.

At the beginning of December 1940, while escorting a convoy west of Ireland, *Saguenay* was torpedoed by the Italian submarine *Argo* and lost her bows. She survived this mishap, but on November 15, 1942, collided with a Panamanian freighter off Cape Race, this time losing her stern. Not considered worth a year's repairs, she spent the remainder of the war as a stationary training ship attached to the shore establishment, H.M.C.S. *Cornwallis.*

SAGUENAY *in October 1940.*

SKEENA (D59) at Plymouth on June 2, 1940. ST. LAURENT is alongside her and RESTIGOUCHE astern.

In the spring of 1944, after more than four years' gruelling service as an ocean escort, *Skeena* became a member of a Canadian support group, Escort Group 12, which saw much action in the Channel during and after D Day. She returned to the North Atlantic that fall, only to be lost on the rocks near Reykjavik, Iceland, on October 25. She was salvaged the following summer by an enterprising Icelander and, presumably, scrapped.

A colleague of *Skeena's* in Escort Group 12, *Assiniboine* had previously seen equally hard service on the North Atlantic. On August 6, 1942 she rammed and sank *U 210* while escorting a convoy. *Restigouche* had a parallel career — several years' unremitting toil as an ocean escort, then a brief but stirring tour of duty with Escort Group 12 in the Channel and the Bay of Biscay in 1944.

RESTIGOUCHE in United Kingdom waters.

Ottawa, which relieved *Restigouche* as a U.K.-based escort in the fall of 1940, joined the Newfoundland Escort Force the following year and was torpedoed and sunk by *U 91* on September 14, 1942.

In September 1940 Canada received six destroyers from an unexpected source — the U.S. Navy. They were among the fifty exchanged by the United States for the use of British bases. Known as the Town class because their Royal Navy names commemorated places common to both Britain and the U.S.A., they had been built toward and after the end of the First World War. Most had four funnels and all were flush-decked, and they were as characteristic of the U.S. Navy between the wars as the corvette would be of the Royal Canadian Navy. Those assigned to Canada were named, with one exception, for U.S.-Canadian boundary rivers: *Columbia, Niagara, St.*

ST. CROIX on June 28, 1942. She exhibits the characteristic modifications made to this class, notably the cut-down funnels and reduced torpedo armament.

Clair, St. Croix and *St. Francis.* The exception was H.M.C.S. *Annapolis.* Two more of this class were acquired later from the Royal Navy — *Hamilton* in 1941 and *Buxton* in 1943. The latter served as a stationary training ship at Cornwallis (moved from Halifax to Deep Brook in 1943).

Annapolis, because she had only three serviceable boilers, was the only Canadian Town class unit never to cross the Atlantic. She spent three and-a-half years as a coastal escort before being placed at the disposal of the shore establishment as a training ship. During most of 1944 she acted as escort, between Halifax and Digby, for the "tame" submarines that assisted in anti-submarine training, and was discarded in 1945.

Columbia and *St. Francis* went to the United Kingdom early in 1941, and for a time were members of Escort Group 4, based at Greenock. Both returned that summer to join the newly-formed Newfoundland Escort Force. On February 25, 1944, while running in fog with faulty radar, *Columbia* ran into a Newfoundland cliff without even touching bottom. With a watertight bulkhead replacing her ruined bow, she was towed to Liverpool, Nova Scotia, to become a fuel and ammunition hulk. *St. Francis* remained on escort duty until the fall of 1943, when she was assigned to training duties.

Niagara and *St. Clair* arrived in the United Kingdom in November 1940 and also became members of Escort Group 4. While in British waters on May 28, 1941 *St. Clair* was subjected to a singularly determined bombing attack. A consort, H.M.S. *Mashona,* was capsized and *St. Clair* picked up her survivors and sank the wreck. She and *Niagara* joined the Newfoundland Escort Force that June, and on August 28 the latter took off the crew of *U 570,* which had surrendered to an attacking R.A.F. bomber. In December 1943,

St. Clair became depot ship to Allied submarines in St. Margaret's Bay, Nova Scotia, and toward the end of 1944 was made a firefighting and damage-control hulk in Bedford Basin. Her remains were still there as late as 1950. *Niagara* became a practice torpedo-firing ship at Halifax in March 1944.

Hamilton was originally intended for the Royal Navy, but was detained by a series of mishaps culminating in grounding off St. John. Offered to Canada because of the long refit in prospect, she finally commissioned in July 1941. After two years' hard escort duty she too was assigned to a shore establishment for training purposes until the war's end.

St. Croix remained on local escort duty until the spring of 1942, when she was assigned to the Newfoundland-Londonderry run, better known as the Newfie-Derry. On July 24, 1942 she attacked and sank *U 90*, and on March 4, 1943, collaborated with corvette H.M.C.S. *Shediac* in the destruction of *U 87.* On September 20 of the same year, however, her luck ran out and she was torpedoed and sunk by *U 305.* Part of her crew was rescued by H.M.S. *Itchen* but the latter was herself torpedoed two days later, with the loss of all but one of *St. Croix's* survivors.

The Town class destroyers, with their narrow beam and excess of tophamper, were inclined to roll appallingly — a feature alleviated in some measure by cutting five feet off their aftermost three funnels, removing all but one set of torpedo tubes and relocating that on the centreline, and removing the two 4-inch guns from their lofty perches abaft the bridge, Whatever their shortcomings, these tired, cranky ships played a vital role in the Battle of the Atlantic, bridging the gap between the destroyer-famine of the days after Dunkirk and the new construction that finally turned the tide in the spring of 1943.

NIAGARA at Halifax in September, 1940, a few days
after being taken over from the U.S. Navy. Formerly
U.S.S. THATCHER, she had as yet undergone no external
modification except for her pendant number. The cable
around her hull is a "degaussing girdle" designed to
protect her against magnetic mines.

In 1940 two Tribal class destroyers were laid down for the Royal Canadian Navy in England at the Tyneside yard of Vickers-Armstrong, and an order for two more followed in 1941. The first two, *Athabaskan* and *Iroquois,* were launched late in 1941, followed by *Haida* and *Huron* in 1942. These were much larger and far better armed than the older River class. Offensive rather than defensive vessels, they spent their wartime careers on the European side of the Atlantic and established impressive service records.

The first ATHABASKAN, *lost in 1944.*

The Canadian Tribals, frequently in company with Royal Navy sisters, saw some of their earliest service on Russian convoys during the winter of 1943-44. *Iroquois* and *Athabaskan* had taken part in patrols of the Bay of Biscay the previous summer and fall, with the object of intercepting U-boats bound to or from their French bases. On August 27, while engaged in this pursuit, *Athabaskan* was hit by a glider bomb and put out of action for more than two months. As members of the Royal Navy's 10th Flotilla all four saw strenuous service and a good deal of action in Biscay and the Channel throughout 1944. The flotilla's duties included anti-submarine patrol, interception of enemy coastal convoys, screening of pre-invasion exercises, and patrol duties connected with the invasion itself.

On the night of April 25-26, 1944, a force including *Athabaskan, Haida* and *Huron* engaged three small German destroyers off the French coast and sank one, *T 29.* Three nights later *Athabaskan* and *Haida* were sent to intercept the other two, *T 24* and *T 27,* bound from St. Malo to Brest for repairs. In the action that ensued *Athabaskan* was torpedoed and sunk. She was avenged half an hour later when *Haida* drove *T 27* ashore.

During the night of June 8-9, 1944, four of the flotilla, including *Haida* and *Huron,* became embroiled with four German destroyers off the coast of Brittany. The Canadian ships forced *Z 32* ashore on the rocks of the Ile de Batz while their consorts finished off *ZH 1.* On June 24 *Haida* and her British sister *Eskimo* jointly destroyed *U 971.*

Iroquois enjoyed particular success in the fall of 1944 against enemy coastal convoys, in partnership with H.M. Ships *Mauritius* and *Ursa.* Through the winter she was occupied on anti-submarine patrol in English coastal waters, but early in 1945 joined her two compatriots in screening aircraft carrier strikes in Norwegian waters. On May 11 *Iroquois* left Rosyth as one of the escort to Crown Prince Olaf, returning to liberated Norway, and shortly thereafter visited Copenhagen, whence she escorted the German cruisers *Prinz Eugen* and *Nürnberg* to Kiel for their formal surrender. *Haida* and *Huron* had meanwhile been paying state visits to Trondheim. The three returned triumphantly to Halifax on June 10, 1945.

SASKATCHEWAN, MICMAC, ST. LAURENT, HURON *and* SIOUX *at Halifax, September 1945. Representatives of three of the R.C.N.'s wartime classes.*

SASKATCHEWAN at sea with a convoy, August 13, 1943.

The Tribals building in 1942 were too thoroughbred to be wasted as plodding convoy escorts. It was correctly foreseen that their speed and gunpower would be required in European waters, and in their place the Canadian escort groups received, between March 1943 and February 1944, six older destroyers from the Royal Navy. These were H.M.C. Ships *Chaudière* (ex-*Hero*), *Gatineau* (ex-*Express*), *Kootenay* (ex-*Decoy*), *Qu'Appelle* (ex-*Foxhound*), *Ottawa* (ex-*Griffin*), and *Saskatchewan* (ex-*Fortune*). Canada's destroyer fleet now presented an admirable cross-section of British construction through the 1930s.

The fortunes of this second group of River class destroyers were singularly interwoven. All but *Chaudière* and *Qu'Appelle* were acquired in the spring of 1943, the latter two commissioning in November 1943 and February 1944. All at first served in one or another of the Canadian escort groups based at Londonderry as part of the Mid-Ocean Escort Force.

Gatineau's experience as escort to convoy ON. 220 demonstrated that the U-boat threat, though greatly diminished by the fall of 1943, was still very real. The convoy, and a slower one that joined it, underwent a five-day attack by 19 U-boats, September 19-23, 1943. Using acoustic torpedoes for the first time, they sank six merchant vessels and three of the escort (including H.M.C.S. *St. Croix*, as we have seen) against the loss of three of their own. The following year *Gatineau* and *Chaudière* were among five Canadian and two Royal Navy escorts to convoy HX.280. *U 744* became the object of a 32-hour hunt to exhaustion by these seven on March 5-6, 1944. Forced at last to surface, the U-boat was scuttled by her crew.

All the River class were withdrawn from the Atlantic at the end of April 1944, for duty in the Channel in support of the impending Normandy landings. Five of them made up the all-Canadian Escort Group 11, which accounted for three U-boats that summer: *Ottawa* and *Kootenay* sank *U 678* in the Channel on July 7, and on August 18 and 20 teamed up with *Chaudière* in the destruction of *U 621* and *U 984* in the Bay of Biscay. Escort Group 11 was disbanded on June 6, 1945, and its component ships, along with others of the River class, had all been disposed of by the end of 1947.

KOOTENAY at Halifax, February 1944.

The last destroyers acquired from the Royal Navy
before the end of the war were two of the "V"
class — smaller than the Tribals but provided
with more modern equipment. They were the first
single-stacked destroyers to serve in the Royal
Canadian Navy. In February and March 1944 they
were commissioned, changing their names,
Valentine and *Vixen,* to *Algonquin* and *Sioux.*
Both saw service in Norwegian waters before
shifting their base to Portsmouth for Channel
patrol duties before D Day and bombardment of
the French coast while the landings were taking
place. With the Allied foothold on the continent

SIOUX, formerly H.M.S. VIXEN.

secure, the two returned to their Scottish base at Scapa Flow, whence they escorted Arctic convoys and screened aircraft carrier operations off the Norwegian coast. It was *Algonquin* that took off 203 unneeded personnel from H.M.C.S. *Nabob* that August, when it appeared that *U 354's* torpedo might have finished her.

The two were placed in reserve after the war, from which sojourn *Sioux* emerged in January 1950 with Squid mortars aft in place of X and Y turrets, and a deckhouse in place of her after torpedo tubes. *Algonquin* was fully modernized as a fast anti-submarine frigate, which entailed stripping her down to the hull, extending the forecastle far aft and fitting a completely new superstructure and bridge. She was also entirely rearmed with weapons designed specifically for anti-submarine work. She recommissioned in February 1953. *Sioux* had meanwhile done two tours of duty in Korean waters before hostilities ended, and would do one more afterward in 1955. She was discarded in 1963 and two years later arrived at La Spezia, Italy, for breaking up. *Algonquin*, finally discarded in 1970, was broken up in Taiwan in 1971.

Four Tribal class destroyers, built at Halifax, were commissioned 1945-48, too late to see action in the Second World War. Their names were: *Athabaskan* (the second of that name), *Cayuga*, *Micmac* and *Nootka*. *Micmac* alone never fired her guns in anger, but spent her life as a training ship. The other three, along with the three survivors of the original quartet, *Iroquois*, *Haida* and *Huron*, all saw much service in Korean waters, 1950-54. In 1964 the last of them was discarded. Only *Haida* escaped the scrapyard, having been purchased from the Crown by Haida Inc., a group of enthusiastic private citizens intent on preserving her. She arrived in Toronto on August 25, 1964, and for some years lay at the

ATHABASKAN (II) coming alongside MAGNIFICENT *on March 24, 1949, during exercises in the Caribbean. As flotilla leader she wears no number.*

foot of York Street; in 1970 she was taken over by the provincial government and given a permanent home at Ontario Place.

Had the Second World War lasted longer, the Canadian Navy would have received a whole flotilla of "C" class destroyers from the Royal Navy, which ultimately built thirty-two of them from 1944 to 1946. As it was, only two, *Crescent* and *Crusader,* were lent to Canada late in 1945, permanent transfer taking place in 1951. Unlike the previous *Crescent* and *Crusader,* these retained their original names. As was the case

HAIDA at her York Street berth, Toronto, in the fall of 1965. Her wartime pendant numbers have been restored and her postwar funnel caps removed, but expense precluded any further restoration to wartime appearance.

with *Algonquin* and *Sioux,* one was fully converted as an anti-submarine frigate, the other only partially. *Crescent's* full transformation, completed in 1956, made her a near-twin to *Algonquin.* Four years later she acquired variable-depth sonar (earlier tried out in *Crusader*) and homing torpedo launchers.

While her sister was being rebuilt, *Crusader* did two tours of duty in the Korean theatre — one before and one after the armistice — totalling nearly two years in those waters. Reverting for a time to a training role, she was placed on the disposal list in 1963. *Crescent* accompanied *Algonquin* to a Taiwan scrapyard in 1971.

ALGONQUIN *after her conversion to anti-submarine frigate — homely but effective.*

CRUSADER as she appeared during her Korean service — little changed except for a funnel cap and new pendant numbers. The shrouded object below 'B' gun is a Hedgehog.

CORVETTES

This class of escort vessel had its origins during the First World War, when William Reed of Smith's Dock Company, near Middlesbrough, Yorkshire, designed the "Z" class whaler for anti-submarine work. Reed's talents were again called upon early in 1939, and again he produced a design based on that of a commercial whale-catcher, specifically his firm's *Southern Pride,* built in 1936. On July 25, 1939, the Admiralty placed with Smith's Dock its first order for the construction of "patrol vessels, whaler type". Winston Churchill, then First Sea Lord, took exception to the designation, and shortly afterward the 18th-century name "corvette" was revived for the new craft.

The Canadian Naval Staff, which had been contemplating a more expensive escort vessel modelled on the British Halcyon class minesweeper, changed its mind on learning of Reed's design, and ordered sixty-four corvettes under the 1939-40 programme. Ten of these were destined for the Royal Navy, but were lent to Canada and manned by Canadian crews for the duration of the European war. These may be distinguished by their names which, like their Royal Navy sisters', were those of flowers. The entire class was known as the Flower class on this account. All the Canadian units however, when completed, were named for towns and cities. Their short length permitted corvettes to pass through the St. Lawrence canal system, making it possible for forty-one of them to be built at Collingwood, Kingston, Midland and Port Arthur.

Of sixteen further units ordered under the 1940-41 programme, the first six were indistinguishable from those built earlier. The other ten were slightly larger owing to their improved design; most notably, they were built with long forecastles, and greater sheer and flare in the bows. (In the earlier model the break in the

WETASKIWIN in 1940, exemplifying the rather "starved" look of a brand-new corvette. In subsequent modifications the forecastle was extended aft, the foremast re-sited abaft the bridge, and the mainmast removed. WETASKIWIN was the first completed of the thirteen west coast-built corvettes.

forecastle was ahead of the bridge, making the waist of these ships extremely wet. This defect was corrected in most of the older units by lengthening the forecastle). The last twenty-seven corvettes built in Canada were of the "increased endurance" type, similar in appearance to their older sisters but having twice the operating range owing to greater fuel capacity. An additional four of these were acquired from Britain in exchange for Canadian-built minesweepers.

The corvettes could, and frequently did, make life thoroughly miserable for their crews. It was said of them that they "would roll in a heavy dew,"

COBOURG, *an "increased endurance" corvette, in the St. Lawrence in 1944.*

BARRIE displaying the corvette's cork-like reaction to a swell. She has had her forecastle extended.

but the buoyancy that made them so lively at sea also gave them comparative immunity to damage from stress of weather. Though not intended as ocean escorts, they filled that role stoutly until the larger frigates came into service toward the end of 1943, and in the process came to typify the Royal Canadian Navy.

On three occasions when Canadian corvettes fought surface actions with U-boats, the enemy craft were boarded. On September 10, 1941, while escorting a convoy, *Chambly* and *Moose Jaw* depth-charged *U 501* to the surface and *Chambly* got a party aboard. The U-boat, whose crew had opened its sea-inlet valves before abandoning it, sank, and no better success attended the efforts of *Oakville's* boarding party to save the mortally-wounded *U 94* south of Haiti on August 28, 1942. At the end of the thirty-two hour hunt of *U 744,* earlier described, it was corvette *Chilliwack* that put a party aboard. Again the prize could not be saved, but the boarders came away with trophies of much interest to naval intelligence.

Of all Canada's warships, the ubiquitous corvette saw by far the most variegated service, as the following brief examination will illustrate.

Only seven of the fourteen corvettes built on the west coast served locally. *Dundas, Edmunston, New Westminster, Quesnel* and *Timmins* were retained there against the possibility of Japanese attack, finally leaving for the Atlantic in September 1942 because they were needed in connection with the North African invasion. The remaining two, *Dawson* and *Vancouver,* helped escort the Attu and Kiska invasion forces in August 1942 and left for the Atlantic the following February.

For various periods between October 1942 and October 1943, seven corvettes *(Fredericton, Halifax, Lethbridge, Oakville, Snowberry, Sudbury*

BRANDON in characteristically scruffy dress. Like WETASKIWIN, she has still the short forecastle and, at the stern, the minesweeping davits that were the hallmark of the earlier corvettes.

and *The Pas)* escorted convoys between New York and Guantanamo, Cuba, under orders of the American Commander, Eastern Sea Frontier. The same seven, plus *Arrowhead, Charlottetown, Hepatica* and *Weyburn,* had, in the spring and summer of 1942, been employed exclusively as escorts to convoys between Halifax and Aruba, in the Dutch East Indies. *Agassiz,* finally, spent July and August 1942 escorting Trinidad convoys.

During and after the North African landings in November 1942, a special series of convoys began running between Britain and the Mediterranean. Sixteen Canadian corvettes were detached to assist in escorting these, and two, *Louisburg* and *Weyburn*, were lost. Similarly in 1944, nineteen of our corvettes were engaged in shepherding coastal convoys to the invasion ports, and escorting cross-Channel traffic in the months after D Day. Again two, *Alberni* and *Regina,* were lost.

In 1944 Canada exchanged twelve new-construction Algerine minesweepers for the same number of Royal Navy Castle class corvettes. The latter, originally named for British castles, received town names in accordance with Canadian practice.

The Castle class corvettes were superior in every way to the original design — forty-five feet longer and slightly beamier, thus providing greatly improved accommodation for their crews. They also had nearly twice the endurance and appreciably better speed. They were armed with a Squid, an ahead-throwing mortar not fitted in any other class of corvette.

All but two of the corvettes *(Sackville* and *Woodstock)* were sold after the war. Some continued their military careers in smaller navies, while others found employment in a variety of mercantile pursuits, including — appropriately — whaling.

War losses:

Alberni — Torpedoed and sunk in the English Channel by *U 480,* August 21, 1944.

Charlottetown — Torpedoed and sunk in the Gulf of St. Lawrence by *U 517,* September 11, 1942.

Lévis — Torpedoed and sunk off Greenland by *U 74* while escorting convoy SC.44, September 19, 1941.

Louisburg — Torpedoed and sunk off Oran by Italian aircraft, February 6, 1943.

Regina — Torpedoed and sunk in the English Channel by *U 667,* August 8, 1944.

Shawinigan — Torpedoed and sunk in Cabot Strait by *U 1228,* November 25, 1944.

Spikenard — Torpedoed and sunk in the western Atlantic by *U 136* while escorting convoy SC. 67, February 11, 1942.

Trentonian — Torpedoed and sunk off Falmouth by *U 1004,* February 22, 1945.

Weyburn — Sunk near Gibraltar by a mine laid by *U 118,* February 22, 1943.

Windflower — Sunk in the north Atlantic in collision with Norwegian S.S. *Zypenberg,* December 7, 1941.

ANTI-SUBMARINE TRAWLERS

In 1941 the British Admiralty had ordered in Canada sixteen anti-submarine trawlers of its numerous Isles class, and on completion in 1942 eight of these were lent to Canada. They were known here as Western Isles trawlers, and bore appropriate names.

Castle class corvette LEASIDE *in June 1945. She was formerly* H.M.S. WALMER CASTLE. *Her Squid mortar is just visible atop the deckhouse in front of the bridge.*

Western Isles trawler ANTICOSTI *September 1942.*

FRIGATES

The unsuitability of the corvette for ocean escort work led to the development in Britain of a larger escort vessel, at first known as the "twin-screw corvette." The design, produced late in 1940 by William Reed, designer of the original corvette, was enthusiastically received in Ottawa, and in 1941 thirty of these craft were ordered. The name "frigate" was, in fact, adopted at the instance of Vice-Admiral Percy Nelles, Canada's Chief of Naval Staff.

Called River class because their Royal Navy counterparts were named for rivers, the Canadian units received town and city names. They were 301 feet long, with two reciprocating corvette engines, designed to drive them at nineteen knots. They had twice the endurance of corvettes, and provided greater space both for the more sophisticated equipment they carried and for the extra crew this required. Thirty-three of these were built under the 1942-43 programme, and twenty-seven under that of 1943-44. A further ten frigates had been built here for Britain, two of which found their way into the U.S. Navy and are said to have been the basis of its destroyer escort design. Seven, identifiable by their river names, were transferred from the Royal Navy in 1944, and with them three Loch class frigates — a slightly larger, improved version designed for prefabrication.

The River class ships were very successful both as convoy escorts and as U-boat hunters, *Swansea* and *Saint John,* for example, each having taken part in the sinking of two U-boats and shared a fifth kill between them. Later units carried twin 4-inch guns, the only Canadian escort ships to do so except the Tribal class destroyers. Beginning in 1943 they were also armed with the Hedgehog, a forward-throwing mortar mounted on the forecastle, which fired a pattern of twenty-four projectiles.

LA HULLOISE in a U.K. port — the only wartime photo yet discovered of this ship.

One of the R.C.N.'s three Loch class frigates, LOCH ALVIE, in Loch Eriboll, Scotland, May 19-20, 1945. Alongside her is U 716 which she escorted part of the way from Norway after the U-boat's surrender.

Looking deceptively small alongside three frigates — U 889 (left) and U 190 at Halifax in September 1945. The frigates are, left to right: JOLIETTE, THETFORD MINES and ST. CATHARINES.

Valleyfield, torpedoed and sunk off Cape Race by U 548 on May 7, 1944, was the only war loss of her class. Chebogue, Magog and Teme, however, were damaged by torpedoes in 1944 and 1945, and not repaired.

A few frigates were retained after the war, and others recommissioned to join them as training ships for officer cadets — the doughty Swansea among them. Between 1953 and 1958 the remaining units of the class underwent a radical conversion from which they emerged flush-decked — the long, low quarterdeck now completely enclosed to provide extra, sheltered working space and to house their newly-acquired Squid anti-submarine mortars. The bridge was also much enlarged and the funnel heightened accordingly. Three other units served the Department of Transport for a time as weather ships, and a fourth, *Stormont,* became unrecognizable under the sleek lines of Aristotle Onassis' yacht, *Christina.*

Of the twenty-one converted units, known as Prestonian class ocean escorts, *Antigonish, Beacon Hill, Buckingham, Cap de la Madeleine, Fort Erie, Inch Arran, Jonquière, La Hulloise, Lanark, Lauzon, New Glasgow, New Waterford, Outremont, Ste. Thérèse, Stettler, Sussexvale* and *Swansea* had been sold for scrap by 1968. Three others, *Penetang, Prestonian* and *Toronto,* were transferred to the Royal Norwegian Navy in 1956. Only *Victoriaville* was left. She had taken over, in 1966, both the duties and the name of the retiring diving tender, *Granby,* and serves as such still.

PENETANG.

60

Aerial view of a Prestonian class unit, NEW GLASGOW.

ARMED YACHTS

Although empowered to requisition British-registered craft of any description from private owners, the Navy failed in 1939 to turn up the hoped-for supply of vessels having potential for anti-submarine use. A clandestine survey of the American yacht market showed promise, but purchase seemed impossible without contravention of neutrality regulations.

It was accordingly arranged for a sufficient number of Canadian yachts, however unpromising, to be requisitioned from their owners, who would then replace them by purchase in the United States. The replacements had, of course, already been selected with care by the Royal Canadian Navy. "Discovering" subsequently that the replacements were better than the yachts originally requisitioned, the navy then took these over instead. By the spring of 1940, fourteen large yachts had been acquired in this somewhat questionable fashion, armed, and given animal names.

Two other large yachts were acquired in 1940. One of them, the *Sans Peur,* had belonged to the Duke of Sutherland; the other, H.M.C.S. *Ambler,* was the only Canadian-registered yacht considered worth taking up. Both retained their own names while in naval service.

Makeshift though the yachts were, they shouldered the responsibility for local anti-submarine defence until the summer of 1941, and proved their worth as training vessels and guardships afterward. *Raccoon,* the only one lost through enemy action, was torpedoed by *U 165* in the St. Lawrence River on September 6, 1942. *Otter* had been destroyed by fire off Halifax on March 26, 1941.

Armed yacht VISON, *formerly the American* AVALON, *a 180-footer built in 1931. 1943 photo.*

DESTROYER ESCORTS

On November 30, 1951, a ship slid off the ways at Canadian Vickers Ltd., Montreal, that was to create a considerable stir in naval circles. Christened *St. Laurent,* she was the prototype of twenty destroyer escorts which entered service 1955-64. The first anti-submarine ships designed and built in Canada, they are striking-looking craft with hulls so smoothly rounded they appear able to follow their quarry underwater. They revive the names of the Canadian River class ships of the Second World War, as well as those of three flush-deckers and a minesweeper. The other three names — *Mackenzie, Terra Nova* and *Yukon* — are new.

The basic design was represented by the seven-unit St. Laurent class, completed 1955-57. Their original armament consisted of two twin 3-inch and two 40-mm. guns, and two Limbo anti-submarine mortar mounts in a well under the quarterdeck. Between 1964 and 1966 all seven emerged from extensive reconstruction, fitted now with a helicopter hangar and flight deck. The former entailed twinning the original single funnel while the latter necessitated the sacrifice of one Limbo mount. All were also fitted with variable-depth sonar (VDS), a Canadian development that denies a submarine the shelter of layers of water at varying depths which tend to confuse fixed sonar systems. The types of weapons carried by these ships make speed of less importance, and they are slow by Second World War standards — about twenty-nine knots. On the other hand, they are much more manoeuverable.

The second group of seven, called the Restigouche class, were completed in 1958-59. They closely resemble the original design, not having been fitted to carry helicopters, but have been modified to incorporate VDS and Jezebel sonar systems — the latter a passive system whereby sonar buoys are dropped and the

CHAUDIERE closely follows the original (1955) DDE configuration. The flat area astern is not a flight deck but the roof of the Limbo mortar well.

submarine located by triangulation. This class
also carries the eight-tube anti-submarine rocket
launcher (ASROC), which enables the quarry to be
attacked at a distance of several miles.

The four Mackenzie class units are essentially a
repeat, completed in 1962-63, of the Restigouches
as originally built. *Annapolis* and *Nipigon*, at first

*ST. LAURENT, the prototype DDE, as rebuilt with paired
funnels and hangar. Her gun is the older American-
pattern, twin 3-inch, 50-calibre model.*

projected as Mackenzies, were completed in 1964 as helicopter carriers (DDHs), incorporating the experience gained in the conversion of the St. Laurents.

The latest DDHs to enter service are the Iroquois class, much larger craft embodying all the weaponry of the earlier classes, and with even

NIPIGON, patterned after the rejuvenated ST. LAURENT, *showing the flight deck and hangar arrangement and VDS gear. Part of the crew is mustered atop the Limbo well.*

MACKENZIE coming alongside a sister — a view chosen to illustrate the DDEs' strikingly rounded lines. Even the anchor is concealed by a door, flush-fitting and almost invisible when closed. The gun is a British pattern, twin 3-inch, 70-calibre model.

more sophisticated electronics. They are the first Canadian ships, apart from the hydrofoil *Bras d'Or*, to be driven by gas turbine engines. The last of the four, *Algonquin,* was commissioned in 1973.

DDH IROQUOIS lands-on one of her Sea King helicopters. Her rather bizarre funnel arrangement is seen to advantage in this aerial view. The recess at the stern houses the VDS towing gear.

HYDROFOIL CRAFT

The earliest practical hydrofoil craft was developed by Alexander Graham Bell and F.W. Baldwin at Baddeck, Nova Scotia. Designated *HD-4,* it was powered by two aircraft engines and air propellers, and in 1919 attained a speed of more than 60 knots.

The Canadian navy's preoccupation with anti-submarine warfare led in the early 1950s to a revival of interest in hydrofoils. A seventeen-ton test vessel, named *Bras d'Or* after the Cape Breton lakes where the *HD-4* was tested, was built in Britain to Naval Research Establishment specifications. It was brought to Halifax aboard the aircraft carrier *Bonaventure* in 1957, and its performance resulted in a feasibility study being carried out by DeHavilland Aircraft of Canada, Ltd., in 1960. The results of the study were promising, and the company was awarded a contract for the ship itself — called a fast hydrofoil escort — in 1963. After some discussion it was decided to name the new vessel *Bras d'Or.* Commissioned in 1968, she ran her first trials in the spring of the following year.

Hull-borne, she is driven by a high-speed, 2400-BHP diesel engine turning twin variable-pitch propellers. At about twenty-three knots her foils lift her hull clear of the water. Foil-borne, she is propelled by a 30,000-SHP gas turbine engine powering twin super-cavitating screws. Trial speeds as high as sixty-three knots were recorded. An automated weapons system, combining miniaturized VDS and homing torpedoes, was designed for the ship but not installed.

Bras d'Or combines, tactically speaking, the seakeeping endurance of a ship with the high-speed capability of an aircraft. She has proved her suitability for service five hundred to a thousand miles offshore, and several of her type could be built for the cost of one DDH. Economy dictated in 1971, however, that she be laid up for a period of five years.

Hydrofoil craft BRAS d'OR *shows her paces at about fifty knots. One of the screws that drive her when "hull-borne" can be seen on the after foil. The forward foil, which carries little weight, is her only steering system. The structure abaft the bridge houses the gas turbine main engine.*

MINE-SWEEPERS

The tiny navy with which Canada entered the war in 1939 numbered four minesweepers among its thirteen ships. These were *Comox, Fundy, Gaspé* and *Nootka* of 1938, Canadian-built copies of the British Basset class minesweeping trawler. *Nootka* became *Nanoose* in 1944, giving up her name to a Tribal class destroyer. Plans to build more of these trawlers were abandoned in favour of a somewhat larger, faster minesweeper being built for the Royal Navy whose prototype was H.M.S. *Bangor.*

The first orders for Canadian Bangors were placed early in 1940, and eighteen were built under the first programme. Twenty sisters followed under two subsequent programmes and six others — built at Vancouver for the Royal Navy but loaned to Canada — made up a total of forty-four steam-driven members of the class. Sixteen of these were built at Toronto and Port Arthur. Like the corvettes, most commemorated towns and cities, but a number were named for bays. As mines were laid in Canadian waters only once — in May 1943 — the Bangors were relegated to the role of escorts to coastal convoys. Sixteen of them, however, had the honour of sweeping the approaches to American beaches for the invasion of Normandy.

Among the Bangors ordered in 1940 were ten with diesel propulsion, smaller and somewhat slower than the regular type. *Brockville, Digby* and *Granby,* of this type, were reactivated after the war as training ships for some time, and *Granby* survived until 1966 as a diving tender. Eighteen of the steam-powered Bangors, sold for scrap after the war, were recovered and placed in strategic reserve in 1951-2. Only two of these, *Kentville* and *Minas,* actually recommissioned and the latter, with nine sisters, was transferred to the Turkish navy in 1958 under the NATO Mutual Aid Program.

NOOTKA, *the minesweeping trawler which gave up her*
name to a destroyer and was thereafter named
NANOOSE.

Bangor class minesweeper CLAYOQUOT, *sunk off Halifax in December 1944.*

*A diesel-engined Bangor, quite different in appearance
from steam-powered members of the class —*
ESQUIMALT, *sunk off Halifax in April 1945 by U 190.*

KAPUSKASING, an Algerine class minesweeper, escorting a convoy in June 1945.

The Bangors were far from ideal in design. Their lack of bow flare made them extremely wet forward in a sea, and it was fortunate that their bridges were enclosed. Living conditions were congested, and tactically they suffered the drawback of short range. These faults were corrected in the Algerine class, of which twelve were built — all at Port Arthur. Much larger, and with much greater endurance and seaworthiness, they were in every way better suited as the convoy escorts they were intended to be. (Although fleet minesweepers by design, the Canadian units had no sweeping gear fitted.) Though easier to build, they could not outperform corvettes as ocean escorts, however, and in 1943 sixteen then building were exchanged with the Royal Navy for corvettes. Most of the original twelve were retained after the war, principally for oceanographic duties, although *Portage, Sault Ste. Marie* and *Wallaceburg* trained reservists on the Great Lakes. *Middlesex* was wrecked on the Nova Scotia coast on December 2, 1946, and the last of her sisters was paid off in 1969.

Two types of wooden-hulled minesweepers were ordered in response to the threat of the magnetic mine. Ten were of the Llewellyn class, of which two were built near Quebec City in 1942 and the rest on the west coast in 1943-44. The other type

LLEWELLYN, *one of ten 105-foot wooden minesweepers.*

were 126-footers with lake names, but none had commissioned by VJ Day and the ten completed were turned over to the U.S.S.R. Six of these were built in Great Lakes boatyards, the other four on the west coast.

Under the 1950 and 1951 programmes, replacements were ordered for the ageing wartime minesweepers. These were the fourteen Bay class coastal minesweepers, which revived the names of some of the Bangors. Six were transferred in 1954 to the French navy but replaced by six of new construction with the same names. These ships are extensively built of aluminum, and bear a close family resemblance to the British Ton class.

War Losses:

Chedabucto — Lost by collision with cable vessel *Lord Kelvin* in the St. Lawrence River, October 21, 1943.

Clayoquot — Torpedoed and sunk off Halifax by *U 806*, December 24, 1944.

Esquimalt — Torpedoed and sunk off Halifax by *U 190*, April 16, 1945.

Guysborough — Torpedoed and sunk off Ushant, in the English Channel, by *U 878*, March 17, 1945.

PINE LAKE, a 126-foot wooden minesweeper, on trials in Georgian Bay in 1945. She and her nine sisters were turned over to the Soviet Union on completion.

Bay class minesweeper RESOLUTE, *launched in 1953.*

SUBMARINES

In August 1914, with war evidently imminent, concern for the security of the British Columbia coast led to a bizarre purchase on the part of the provincial government. Informed that two submarines originally intended for the Chilean government were for sale at Seattle, the premier, Sir Richard McBride, purchased them on his own authority. A rendezvous was arranged just outside Canadian territorial waters, and there the transfer of the two boats took place. They arrived at Esquimalt on August 5, less than a day after the outbreak of war. Luckily for Sir Richard, the Dominion government ratified his purchase, and on August 7 the Royal Canadian Navy had its first submarines. As they were similar to the Royal Navy's "C" class, they were designated *CC 1* and *CC 2.*

After nearly three years on the west coast, where they exemplified the "fleet in being" principle on a miniscule scale, the boats were ordered to the war zone, and in June 1917 set out for Halifax. Accompanied by their mother ship *Shearwater,* they passed through the Panama Canal in August — the first ships ever to do so under the White Ensign — and arrived at Halifax on October 14. In the end they were allowed to remain on this side of the Atlantic as training craft, and were sold for scrap in 1920.

During the First World War, ten "H" class submarines were built at Montreal and an equal number at Groton, Connecticut, for the Royal Navy. Two of the U.S.-built boats, *H 14* and *H 15,* were en route for Britain when the war ended, and were ordered to Bermuda. Offered to Canada, they commissioned at Halifax in June 1919 as *CH 14* and *CH 15.* They were laid up in 1922 and in 1927 sold, along with the cruiser *Aurora.* It was to be eighteen years before the Canadian navy again commissioned submarines.

Submarines CC 1 and CC 2 at Halifax about 1918. The ship in background is the patrol vessel CARTIER.

Submarines CH 14 and CH 15, perhaps celebrating Dominion Day.

On May 12 and 13, 1945, *U 190* and *U 889* surrendered to Canadian units, hostilities having ended a few days previously. Both were of the large IX C type, built at Bremen in 1942 and 1944. They were commissioned in the Royal Canadian Navy on May 14 for testing and evaluation, after which, on January 12, 1946, *U 889* was turned over to the U.S. Navy. *U 190* was decommissioned in July 1947, and on October 21 of that year was sunk by Canadian naval aircraft near the position where she had sunk H.M.C.S. *Esquimalt* a year and-a-half earlier.

*U 889, just before her formal surrender to the R.C.N.
off Shelburne, N.S., May 13, 1945. The great size of the
IX C boats can be appreciated, as well as their
formidable anti-aircraft armament. The tube on the side
of the conning tower connected the Snorkel mast,
when raised, with the interior of the boat, enabling her
to run on diesels while submerged.*

During and after the war it had been the custom of the Royal Navy to provide a resident submarine for anti-submarine training off Halifax. By 1961, with a growing fleet of new anti-submarine ships stationed at Esquimalt, it had become essential to have a submarine stationed there. U.S.S. *Burrfish* was accordingly borrowed and commissioned at New London, Connecticut, as H.M.C.S. *Grilse* — a name last borne by an armed yacht in the First World War. *Burrfish,* launched in 1943, had seen service in the Pacific and had been converted in 1949 for duty as a radar picket submarine.

Grilse was replaced in 1968 by *Rainbow,* purchased from the U.S. Navy, for which she had been launched in 1944 as *Argonaut.* Originally a near-sister to *Grilse,* she had undergone modernization in 1952 to what the U.S. Navy calls Guppy configuration. *Rainbow* was paid off at the end of 1974.

In 1965 H.M.C.S. *Ojibwa* was commissioned, the first submarine built to Canadian order. Two sisters, *Onondaga* and *Okanagan,* followed in 1967 and 1968. All were built in Britain, at Chatham Dockyard, and are duplicates of the Royal Navy's Oberon class, its latest conventionally-powered submarines.

GRILSE, As U.S.S. BURRFISH, she served in the Pacific during the Second World War.

RAINBOW, a near-sister to GRILSE, *displays the faired-over conning tower and "sail" characteristic of U.S.N. "Guppy" conversion.*

OJIBWA. *The dome on her bow houses a sonar transducer.*

MOTOR CRAFT

A dramatic and intensely personal kind of war was waged in the English Channel, 1940-45, between Britain's coastal forces and their German counterparts from bases in occupied France, Belgium and Holland. The British crews fought principally in motor torpedo boats and motor gunboats, while the Germans used a larger, faster type known to the Allies as an E-boat.

The proposal, made as early as 1942, that Canada should form a British-based flotilla of motor craft was not acted upon because we had no such boats. A year later, however, the Admiralty offered to supply boats if the Canadians would man them. Two flotillas were accordingly formed early in 1944: the 29th, equipped with seventy-two foot "G" type motor torpedo boats, and the 65th, with 115-foot Fairmile "D" type boats. These took part in a variety of pre-invasion operations off the French coast, and in protecting the flank of the invading forces. After D Day they helped prevent E-boats and larger craft from attacking Cross-Channel traffic replenishing the beachhead. 29th Flotilla *MTBs 460* and *463* fell prey to mines on July 1 and 7, 1944, and five more — MTBs *459, 461, 462, 465* and *466* — were destroyed by fire at Ostend, Belgium, on February 14, 1945.

Between 1941 and 1944, eighty Fairmile "B" type motor launches were built at eleven Canadian boatyards. Seven of these, located on the Great Lakes, turned out fifty-nine of the boats, while fourteen of the remainder were built on the west coast and seven at Weymouth, Nova Scotia. They were numbered *ML 050* to *ML 129.*

These Fairmiles were intended as escorts to St. Lawrence River and coastal convoys, and as port-defence craft. Though neither fast enough nor manoeuverable enough to be good anti-submarine vessels, they performed tasks that would otherwise have occupied larger ships urgently needed elsewhere. Most were sold at

MTB 459 in the English Channel, May 29, 1944. One of her 18'' torpedo tubes is visible abreast the bridge. The gun forward is a power-operated 2-pounder.

Bristling with weapons, MTB 745 had four torpedo tubes. One may be seen aft, the other partially concealed below the bridge. The hull is "scooped out" so as to give clearance to the latter's torpedo when fired.

war's end, but half a dozen still served as training craft on the Great Lakes in the late 1950s: *Beaver* (ex-*ML 106*), *Cougar* (ex-*ML 104*), *Moose* (ex-*ML 111*), *Raccoon* (ex-*ML 079*), *Reindeer* (ex-*ML 116*), and *Wolf* (ex-*ML 062*). A seventh, *Elk* (ex-*ML 124*) served on the west coast. These had received their Canadian animal names in 1954.

ML 121 leads the surrendered U 889 into Shelburne, May 13, 1945.

ARCTIC PATROL VESSEL

H.M.C.S. *Labrador* was built in recognition of the growing strategic importance of Canada's Arctic regions, and with a view to the assertion of our sovereignty there. Her design was adapted from that of the U.S. Coast Guard's Wind class of icebreakers. Like them, she was built for power rather than speed, and her six diesel-electric engines drive her at a top speed of sixteen knots. Heeling tanks connected by reversible-propeller type pumps enable water ballast to be hurled from side to side at 40,000 gallons per minute, so she can rock herself free when beset by ice. She carries two helicopters.

Commissioned in 1954, *Labrador* sailed that summer on the first of four voyages she would make to the Arctic as a naval vessel. On that voyage she became the first warship to negotiate the Northwest Passage across the top of this continent and, returning to Halifax via the Panama Canal, the first to circumnavigate North America. On *Labrador's* second voyage, in 1955, she transported personnel and equipment for the construction of the eastern portion of the U.S.-Canadian Distant Early Warning (DEW) Line. That summer and the next, she also carried out extensive hydrographic surveys in the eastern Arctic — spending five and one-half months there in 1956 alone. A departure from custom in 1957 found her across the Atlantic, paying visits to Portsmouth, Oslo and Copenhagen, and that November she was paid off for refit.

Looking oddly toy-like, LABRADOR sits for her portrait against an iceberg backdrop in 1954, while making her way through the Northwest Passage.

She was fated not to fly the White Ensign again, for the decision was taken to transfer her to the Department of Transport. As C.C.G.S. *Labrador,* she is now primarily used as an icebreaker in the lower St. Lawrence, but still continues to embark scientists for summer studies in the Arctic.

OPERATIONAL SUPPORT SHIPS

The first of this type, H.M.C.S. *Provider,* was commissioned in 1963. The largest ship hitherto built in Canada for the Royal Canadian Navy, she gave its ships for the first time the ability to stay at sea for extended periods, greatly increasing their mobility and range. She has stowage space for some 12,000 tons of fuel oil, diesel oil and aviation gasoline, as well as for spare parts, ammunition and missiles, general stores and foods.

Experience with *Provider* led to a modified design in the next two support ships, commissioned in 1969 and 1970. Though similar in size, these twin sisters, H.M.C.S. *Preserver* and *Protecteur,* are strikingly different in appearance. Most notable, apart from their higher freeboard and massive bridge structures, are the paired funnels, which make possible wider hangar doors. Two fifteen-ton cranes aft enhance their sealift capability for heavy vehicles, and cargo can be handled with great ease and speed. Unlike *Provider,* too, the newer pair are armed with a twin 3-inch gun and have provision for a Sea Sparrow anti-aircraft missile launcher.

All three ships can replenish other fleet units at twenty knots, with automatic tensioning equipment to compensate for the ships' motion as fuel oil is transferred at twenty-five tons per minute. Each can carry three anti-submarine helicopters as spares for the fleet or for transferring pallet loads of supplies from ship to ship.

Provider and *Preserver* revive the names of Fairmile depot ships completed in 1942, while *Protecteur* recalls, with a French accent, H.M.C.S. *Protector,* the wartime naval base at Sydney, Nova Scotia.

*But for her derrick-like transfer rigs and large hangar
and flight deck aft,* PROVIDER *would look very much like
an ordinary tanker.*

PROTECTEUR is notable for her massive bridge, paired funnels and twin 3-inch "bow chaser." The low structure ahead of the bridge is designed to house a Sea Sparrow missile launcher if required.

APPENDIX

The commissioning dates in this appendix have for the most part been taken from Tucker's *The Naval Service of Canada,* Volume 2. Tucker's "disposal" dates contain many inconsistencies, however, and the paying-off dates from Schull's *The Far Distant Ships* have been substituted in hopes of presenting a more accurate picture. Corresponding dates for ships which survived into the post-war period, or were built since 1945, have been obtained from official sources.

Some ships were brought out of reserve during the Korean emergency of the early '50s; others, sold for conversion or scrapping, were actually repurchased. The dates of service given do not take note of the hiatus in their careers, or in those of ships decommissioned while undergoing major reconstruction.

With respect to ships' particulars, it should be noted that dimensions have been rounded off to the nearest foot. In the case of submarines, both displacement and speed appear in a surfaced/submerged format. An officers/men format has been adopted, where possible, for complement, but these figures are at best approximate in any case.

Under armament, the first number represents the total number of barrels or tubes. If individual weapons had more than one, the number per mounting follows in parentheses. For example, 9-6" (3 x III), signifies that the ship carried three triple 6-inch turrets. AA means Anti-Aircraft, TT means Torpedo Tubes. It has not been thought necessary to state that almost all fighting units below cruiser size were supplied with depth charges.

Pendant numbers were worn by all escort ships up to and including destroyers, and served to distinguish one member of a numerous class from another. As well as appearing on both sides of the forecastle and on the stern, they were displayed in the form of flags. Presumably no further greeting would have been necessary had fate brought together H.M.S. *Hartland* (YOO) and H.M.C.S. *Restigouche* (HOO)!

Missing numbers in the series on pages 110-111 are accounted for by the fact that numbers were allocated to all British and Commonwealth ships from one list, whose "K" section alone contained nearly 700 names. Where two pendant numbers are shown on pages 99-109, the first is the wartime one, the second that assigned after 1949. Exceptions are *Saguenay, Skeena* and *Assiniboine,* whose 'D' flag superior was changed to 'I' in 1940.

Name	Pendant No.		Displacement (tons)	Dimensions (feet)	Top Speed (knots)	Crew	Dates of Service in RCN Commissioned	Paid Off	Armament	Remarks
Cruisers (5)										
RAINBOW			3,600	314 x 43 x 18	17	c.300	4.8.10	1.6.20	2-6", 6-4.7", 2-14" TT	Launched in 1891
NIOBE			11,000	450 x 69 x 26	17	c.700	6.9.10	31.5.20	16-6", 12-12 pdrs., 2-18" TT	Launched in 1897
AURORA			3,512	436 x 39 x 14	29	370	1.11.20	1.7.22	2-6", 6-4", 8-21" TT (4 x II)	Launched in 1913
QUEBEC (ex-*Uganda*)	66	31	8,800	555 x 62 x 17	30	c.730	21.10.44	13.6.56	9-6" (3 x III), 8-4" (4 x II), 6-21" TT (2 x III) Numerous 20 and 40 mm.	
ONTARIO (ex-*Minotaur*)	53	32	8,800	555 x 63 x 17	30	c.730	26.4.45	15.10.58	9-6" (3 x III), 10-4" (5 x II), 6-21" TT (2 x III) Numerous 20 and 40 mm.	
Armed Merchant Cruisers (3)										
PRINCE DAVID	F89		5,736	385 x 57 x 21	22	31/386	28.12.40	6.45	4-4" (2 x II). 2-2 pdrs. 8-20 mm.	All three launched in 1930 Armament cited is for *Prince David* and *Prince Henry* as converted to Infantry Landing Ships; for *Prince Robert* as A/A Ship.
PRINCE HENRY	F70		5,736	385 x 57 x 21	22	31/386	4.12.40	15.4.45	4-4" (2 x II), 2-2 pdrs., 8-20 mm.	
PRINCE ROBERT	F56		5,675	385 x 57 x 21	22	33/405	31.7.40	10.12.45	10-4" (5 x II), 2-2 pdrs., 6-20 mm.	Original armament: 4-6", 2-3"
Aircraft Carriers (5)										
NABOB	D77		15,390	495 x 69 x 25	18	c.1,000	7.9.43	10.10.44	2-5", 16-40 mm. (8 x II), 20-20 mm. Aircraft: 20	Laid down as merchant ships at Tacoma, Wash., *Nabob* in 1942 as *Edisto*, *Puncher* in 1943 as *Willapa*.
PUNCHER	D79		14,170	492 x 69 x 25	18	c.1,000	5.2.44	16.1.46	Same as *Nabob*.	
WARRIOR		31 (RN)	13,350	695 x 80 x 21	24	c.1,000	24.1.46	23.3.48	24-2 pdr. (6 x IV), 19-40 mm. Aircraft: 30	
MAGNIFICENT		21 (RN)	14,000	695 x 80 x 24	24	c.1,000	7.4.48	14.6.57	6-40 mm. (3 x II), 18-40 mm. (single) Aircraft: 30	
BONAVENTURE (ex-*Powerful*)		22	16,000	704 x 80 x 24	24	c.1,000	17.1.57	1.7.70	8-3" (4 x II) Aircraft: 30	Launched in 1945
Destroyers										
PATRICIAN			1,004	271 x 27 x 11	35	80	1.11.20	1.1.28	3-4", 1-2 pdr. 4-21" TT (2 x II)	*Patrician* and *Patriot* launched in 1916
PATRIOT			1,004	271 x 27 x 11	35	80	1.11.20	21.10.27	Same as *Patrician*	
CHAMPLAIN (ex-*Torbay*)			1,075	275 x 27 x 11	36	90	1.3.28	25.11.36	3-4", 1-2 pdr. 4-21" TT (2 x II)	*Torbay* and *Toreador* launched in 1918
VANCOUVER (ex-*Toreador*)			1,075	275 x 27 x 11	36	90	1.3.28	25.11.36	Same as *Champlain*	
SAGUENAY	D79	I79	1,337	320 x 32 x 11	31	10/171	22.5.31	30.7.45	4-4.7" 8-21" TT (2 x IV)	
SKEENA	D59	I59	1,337	320 x 32 x 11	31	10/171	10.6.31	25.10.44	Modified to: 2-4.7", 1-3" AA 4-21" TT, 6-20 mm.	

	Displacement (tons)	Dimensions (feet)	Top Speed (knots)	Crew	Armament	Remarks
RIVER Class (12) ex-Royal Navy	1,360 average	329 x 33 x 11	31	10/171	4-4.7" 8-21" TT (2 x IV) Modified to: 2 or 3-4.7", 1-3" AA 4-21" TT, 6-20 mm. Hedgehog	*Assiniboine* and the former C class units were all launched in 1931, D class units in 1932, E and F class units in 1934, and G and H class units in 1935 and 1936.

	Pendant No.		Commissioned	Paid Off		Pendant No.	Commissioned	Paid Off
ASSINIBOINE (ex-Kempenfelt)	D18	I18	19.10.39	8.8.45	OTTAWA (ex-Crusader)	H60	15.6.38	14.9.42
CHAUDIERE (ex-Hero)	H99		15.11.43	12.8.45	OTTAWA (II) (ex-Griffin)	H31	20.3.43	1.11.45
FRASER (ex-Crescent)	H48		17.2.37	25.6.40	QU'APPELLE (ex-Foxhound)	H69	8.2.44	11.10.45
GATINEAU (ex-Express)	H61		3.6.43	10.1.46	RESTIGOUCHE (ex-Comet)	H00	15.6.38	5.10.45
KOOTENAY (ex-Decoy)	H75		12.4.43	26.10.45	SASKATCHEWAN (ex-Fortune)	H70	31.5.43	28.1.46
MARGAREE (ex-Diana)	H49		6.9.40	22.10.40	ST. LAURENT (ex-Cygnet)	H83	17.2.37	10.10.45

	Displacement (tons)	Dimensions (feet)	Top Speed (knots)	Crew	Armament	Remarks
TOWN Class (8)	1,100 average	314 x 31 x 12	28	10/143	1-4', 1-12 pdr. AA 3-21" TT (1 x III) 4-20 mm., Hedgehog	All were launched in 1918 except *St. Croix* and *St. Francis,* launched in 1919. As originally armed, they had 5-4" and 1-3" guns, and 12-21" TT (4 x III)

	Pendant No.	Commissioned	Paid Off		Pendant No.	Commissioned	Paid Off
ANNAPOLIS (ex-USS Mackenzie)	I04	24.9.40	4.6.45	NIAGARA (ex-USS Thatcher)	I57	24.9.40	15.9.45
BUXTON (ex-USS Edwards)	H96	4.11.43	2.6.45	ST. CLAIR (ex-USS Williams)	I65	24.9.40	23.8.44
COLUMBIA (ex-USS Haraden)	I49	24.9.40	12.6.45	ST. CROIX (ex-USS McCook)	I81	24.9.40	20.9.43
HAMILTON (ex-USS Kalk)	I24	6.7.41	8.6.45	ST. FRANCIS (ex-USS Bancroft)	I93	24.9.40	11.6.45

	Displacement (tons)	Dimensions (feet)	Top Speed (knots)	Crew	Armament	Remarks
TRIBAL Class (8)	1,950 average	377 x 36 x 9	36	14/245	6-4.7" (3 x II) 2-4" AA (1 x II) 4-2 pdr. pompom (1 x IV) 6-20 mm. 4-21" TT (1 x IV) Modified post-war to: 4-4" (2 x II) 2-3" (1 x II), 4-40 mm. 4-21" TT (1 x IV) 2 Squid	

	Pendant No.		Commissioned	Paid Off
ATHABASKAN	G07		3.2.43	29.4.44
ATHABASKAN (II)	R79	219	20.1.48	21.4.66
CAYUGA	R04	218	20.10.47	27.2.64
HAIDA	G63	215	30.8.43	11.10.63
HURON	G24	216	19.7.43	30.4.63
IROQUOIS	G89	217	30.11.42	24.10.62
MICMAC	R10	214	12.9.45	31.3.64
NOOTKA (II)	R96	213	7.8.46	6.2.64

	Displacement (tons)	Dimensions (feet)	Top Speed (knots)	Crew		Armament	Remarks
"V" and "C" Classes (4)	1,710	363 x 36 x 10	31	c.200		"V" Class: 4-4.7" 4-40 mm., 4-20 mm. 8-21" TT (2 x IV) "C" Class: 4-4.5" 4-40 mm., 4-20 mm. 4-21" TT (1 x IV)	Post-war armament (*Algonquin* and *Crescent*): 2-4" (1 x II), 2-3" (1 x II) 2-40 mm. 1 Limbo Homing torpedoes. *Crusader*: 3-4.5", 6-40 mm. 4-21" TT (I x IV) *Sioux*: 2-4.7", 6-40 mm. 4-21" TT (1 x IV) 2 Squid

	Pendant No.		Commissioned	Paid Off
ALGONQUIN (ex-Valentine)	R17	224	17.2.44	1.4.70
SIOUX (ex-Vixen)	R64	225	21.2.44	30.10.63
CRESCENT	R16	226	10.9.45	1.4.70
CRUSADER	R20	228	15.11.45	15.1.60

Destroyer Escorts

	Displacement (tons)	Dimensions (feet)	Top Speed (knots)	Crew	Armament
ST. LAURENT Class DDEs (7)	2,263	366 x 42 x 13	28	11/198	4-3" (2 x II) 2-40 mm. 2 Limbo Homing torpedoes

	Pendant No.	Commissioned	Paid Off
ASSINIBOINE (II)	DDE 234	16.8.56	
FRASER (II)	233	28.6.57	
MARGAREE (II)	230	5.10.57	
OTTAWA (III)	229	10.11.56	
SAGUENAY (II)	206	15.12.56	
ST. LAURENT (II)	205	29.10.55	14.6.74
SKEENA (II)	207	30.3.57	

	Displacement (tons)	Dimensions (feet)	Top Speed (knots)	Crew	Armament
RESTIGOUCHE Class DDEs (7)	2,366	371 x 42 x 14	28	9/200	2-3" (1 x II) 2-40 mm. 1 Limbo 1 ASROC Homing torpedoes

	Pendant No.	Commissioned	Paid Off
CHAUDIERE (II)	DDE 235	14.11.59	23.5.74
COLUMBIA (II)	260	7.11.59	18.2.74
GATINEAU (II)	236	17.2.59	
KOOTENAY (II)	258	7.3.59	
RESTIGOUCHE (II)	257	7.6.58	
ST. CROIX (II)	256	4.10.58	
TERRA NOVA	259	6.6.59	

	Displacement (tons)	Dimensions (feet)	Top Speed (knots)	Crew	Armament
MACKENZIE Class DDHs (4)	2,380	366 x 42 x 13	28	11/198	4-3" (2 x II) 2 Limbo Homing torpedoes

	Pendant No.	Commissioned	Paid Off
MACKENZIE	DDH 261	6.10.62	
QU'APPELLE (II)	264	14.9.63	
SASKATCHEWAN (II)	262	16.2.63	
YUKON	263	25.5.63	

	Displacement (tons)	Dimensions (feet)	Top Speed (knots)	Crew	Armament
ANNAPOLIS Class DDHs (2)	2,400	371 x 42 x 14	28	11/225	2-3" (1 x II) 1 Limbo Homing torpedoes 1 Sea King helicopter

	Pendant No.	Commissioned	Paid Off
ANNAPOLIS (II)	DDH 265	19.12.64	
NIPIGON (II)	266	30.5.64	

	Displacement (tons)	Dimensions (feet)	Top Speed (knots)	Crew	Armament
IROQUOIS Class DDHs (4)	4,050 *full load*	426 x 50 x 14	27	63/274	1-5" 1-A/S Mortar Homing torpedoes 2 Sea King helicopters

	Pendant No.	Commissioned	Paid Off
ALGONQUIN (II)	DDH 283	3.11.73	
ATHABASKAN (III)	282	30.9.72	
HURON (II)	281	16.12.72	
IROQUOIS (II)	280	29.7.72	

Fast Hydrofoil Escort

		Displacement (tons)	Dimensions (feet)	Top Speed (knots)	Crew	Commissioned	Paid Off	Armament
BRAS d'OR (II)	FHE 400	180	151 x 21 x 23	60	4/25	19.7.68	1.5.72	nil

Corvettes

	Displacement (tons)	Dimensions (feet)	Top Speed (knots)	Crew	Armament
FLOWER Class, 1939-40 Programme (64)	950	205 x 33 x 13	16	6/79	1-4", 2-20 mm. 1-2 pdr. Hedgehog in many.

	Pendant No.	Commissioned	Paid Off		Pendant No.	Commissioned	Paid Off
AGASSIZ	K129	23.1.41	9.1.45	EYEBRIGHT	K150	26.11.40	7.7.45
ALBERNI	K103	4.2.41	21.8.44	FENNEL	K194	15.1.41	12.6.45
ALGOMA	K127	11.7.41	10.7.45	GALT	K163	15.5.41	26.6.45
AMHERST	K148	5.8.41	11.7.45	HEPATICA	K159	12.11.40	15.7.45
ARROWHEAD	K145	21.11.40	4.7.45	KAMLOOPS	K176	17.3.41	30.6.45
ARVIDA	K113	22.5.41	24.6.45	KAMSACK	K171	4.10.41	24.7.45
BADDECK	K147	18.5.41	7.7.45	KENOGAMI	K125	29.6.41	11.7.45
BARRIE	K138	12.5.41	19.9.44	LETHBRIDGE	K160	25.6.41	18.7.45
BATTLEFORD	K165	31.7.41	20.7.45	LEVIS	K115	16.5.41	19.9.41
BITTERSWEET	K182	23.1.41	22.6.45	LOUISBURG	K143	29.9.41	6.2.43
BRANDON	K149	22.7.41	26.4.45	LUNENBURG	K151	4.12.41	18.7.45
BUCTOUCHE	K179	5.6.41	17.6.45	MATAPEDIA	K112	9.5.41	20.7.45
CAMROSE	K154	30.6.41	18.7.45	MAYFLOWER	K191	9.11.40	31.5.45
CHAMBLY	K116	18.12.40	29.8.45	MONCTON	K139	24.4.42	12.12.45
CHICOUTIMI	K156	12.5.41	26.11.44	MOOSE JAW	K164	19.6.41	26.8.45
CHILLIWACK	K131	8.4.41	9.7.45	MORDEN	K170	6.9.41	3.7.45
COBALT	K124	25.11.40	5.7.45	NANAIMO	K101	26.4.41	27.9.45
COLLINGWOOD	K180	9.11.40	16.7.45	NAPANEE	K118	12.5.41	16.7.45
DAUPHIN	K157	17.5.41	24.6.45	OAKVILLE	K178	18.11.41	16.7.45
DAWSON	K104	6.10.41	15.6.45	ORILLIA	K119	29.4.41	18.7.45
DRUMHELLER	K167	13.9.41	5.7.45	PICTOU	K146	29.4.41	16.7.45
DUNVEGAN	K177	9.9.41	6.7.45	PRESCOTT	K161	26.6.41	17.7.45
EDMUNSTON	K106	21.10.41	20.6.45	QUESNEL	K133	23.5.41	28.6.45

	Pendant No.	Commissioned	Paid Off		Pendant No.	Commissioned	Paid Off
RIMOUSKI	K121	26.4.41	12.6.45	SPIKENARD	K198	8.12.40	10.2.42
ROSTHERN	K169	17.6.41	16.7.45	SUDBURY	K162	15.10.41	19.6.45
SACKVILLE	K181	30.12.41	8.4.46	SUMMERSIDE	K141	11.9.41	2.7.45
SASKATOON	K158	9.6.41	3.7.45	THE PAS	K168	21.10.41	24.6.45
SHAWINIGAN	K136	19.9.41	24.11.44	TRAIL	K174	30.4.41	12.7.45
SHEDIAC	K110	8.7.41	19.8.45	TRILLIUM	K172	31.10.40	16.7.45
SHERBROOKE	K152	5.6.41	25.6.45	WETASKIWIN	K175	17.12.40	16.6.45
SNOWBERRY	K166	30.11.40	8.6.45	WEYBURN	K173	26.11.41	22.2.43
SOREL	K153	19.8.41	20.6.45	WINDFLOWER	K155	20.10.40	7.12.41

Corvettes

FLOWER Class,
1940-41 Programme (6)   Particulars same as those of the 1939-40 Programme

	Pendant No.	Commissioned	Paid Off		Pendant No.	Commissioned	Paid Off
BRANTFORD	K218	15.5.42	17.7.45	NEW WESTMINSTER	K228	31.1.42	3.9.45
DUNDAS	K229	1.4.42	20.7.45	TIMMINS	K223	10.2.42	10.7.45
MIDLAND	K220	8.11.41	11.7.45	VANCOUVER (II)	K240	20.3.42	22.6.45

Revised FLOWER Class, 1940-41 Programme (10)	1,015	208 x 33 x 15	16	6/79		Armament same as that of the 1939-40 Programme.	

	Pendant No.	Commissioned	Paid Off		Pendant No.	Commissioned	Paid Off
CALGARY	K231	16.12.41	19.6.45	LA MALBAIE	K273	28.4.42	2.7.45
CHARLOTTETOWN	K244	13.12.41	11.9.42	PORT ARTHUR	K233	26.5.42	11.7.45
FREDERICTON	K245	8.12.41	3.10.45	REGINA	K234	22.1.42	11.9.44
HALIFAX	K237	26.11.41	10.7.45	VILLE de QUEBEC	K242	24.5.42	3.7.45
KITCHENER	K225	28.6.42	16.7.45	WOODSTOCK	K238	1.5.42	18.3.46

Revised FLOWER Class, Increased Endurance, 1942-43 Programme (15)	970	208 x 33 x 16	16	6/79		Armament same as that of the 1939-40 Programme.	

	Pendant No.	Commissioned	Paid Off		Pendant No.	Commissioned	Paid Off
ATHOLL	K 15	14.10.43	19.7.45	NORSYD	K520	22.12.43	21.6.45
COBOURG	K333	11.5.44	16.7.45	NORTH BAY	K339	25.10.43	4.7.45
FERGUS	K686	18.11.44	9.7.45	OWEN SOUND	K340	17.11.43	14.7.45
FRONTENAC	K335	26.10.43	17.7.45	RIVIERE du LOUP	K357	21.11.43	5.7.45
GUELPH	K687	9.5.44	30.6.45	ST. LAMBERT	K343	27.5.44	20.8.45
HAWKESBURY	K415	14.6.44	7.7.45	TRENTONIAN	K368	1.12.43	22.2.45
LINDSAY	K338	15.11.43	23.7.45	WHITBY	K346	6.6.44	12.7.45
LOUISBURG (II)	K401	13.12.43	21.6.45				

Revised FLOWER Class, Increased Endurance, 1943-44 Programme (12)

Particulars same as those of the 1942-43 Programme

	Pendant No.	Commissioned	Paid Off		Pendant No.	Commissioned	Paid Off
ASBESTOS	K358	16.6.44	4.7.45	PETERBOROUGH	K342	1.6.44	20.8.45
BEAUHARNOIS	K540	25.9.44	24.7.45	SMITHS FALLS	K345	28.11.44	4.7.45
BELLEVILLE	K332	19.10.44	8.7.45	STELLARTON	K457	29.9.44	4.7.45
LACHUTE	K440	26.10.44	6.7.45	STRATHROY	K455	20.11.44	6.7.45
MERRITTONIA	K688	10.11.44	19.8.45	THORLOCK	K394	13.11.44	10.7.45
PARRY SOUND	K341	30.8.44	7.7.45	WEST YORK	K369	6.10.44	9.7.45

Revised FLOWER Class, Increased Endurance, ex-Royal Navy (4)

Particulars same as those of the 1942-43 Programme

	Pendant No.	Commissioned	Paid Off		Pendant No.	Commissioned	Paid Off
FOREST HILL (ex-*Ceanothus*)	K486	1.12.43	17.9.44	LONG BRANCH (ex-*Candytuft*)	K487	5.11.44	14.6.45
GIFFARD (ex-*Buddleia*)	K402	10.11.43	8.7.45	MIMICO (ex-*Bulrush*)	K485	8.2.44	19.7.45

CASTLE Class ex-Royal Navy (12)   1,060   252 x 37 x 15   16.5   7 / 105   1-4", 2-20 mm. 1 Squid

	Pendant No.	Commissioned	Paid Off		Pendant No.	Commissioned	Paid Off
ARNPRIOR (ex-*Rising Castle*)	K494	8.6.44	6.3.46	KINCARDINE (ex-*Tamworth Castle*)	K490	19.6.44	13.9.45
BOWMANVILLE (ex-*Nunney Castle*)	K493	28.9.44	24.8.45	LEASIDE (ex-*Walmer Castle*)	K492	21.8.44	20.11.45
COPPER CLIFF (ex-*Hever Castle*)	K495	25.7.44	20.9.45	ORANGEVILLE (ex-*Hedingham Castle*)	K491	24.4.44	16.10.45
HESPELER (ex-*Guildford Castle*)	K489	28.2.44	24.8.45	PETROLIA (ex-*Sherborne Castle*)	K498	29.6.44	25.6.45
HUMBERSTONE (ex-*Norham Castle*)	K497	6.9.44	14.10.45	ST. THOMAS (ex-*Sandgate Castle*)	K488	4.5.44	22.11.45
HUNTSVILLE (ex-*Woolvesey Castle*)	K499	6.6.44	9.9.45	TILLSONBURG (ex-*Pembroke Castle*)	K496	29.6.44	28.11.45

Frigates

RIVER Class, 1942-43 Programme (33)   1,445   301 x 37 x 14   19   8 / 133

2-4" (1 x II)
4-20 mm.
Hedgehog

Prestonian class armament:
2-4" (1 x II)
2-40 mm. (1 x II)
4-40 mm. singles
2 Limbo

	Pendant No.		Commissioned	Paid Off		Pendant No.		Commissioned	Paid Off
BEACON HILL	K407	303	16.5.44	15.9.67					
CAP de la MADELEINE	K663	317	30.9.44	15.5.65	NEW GLASGOW	K320	315	23.12.43	6.12.66
CAPE BRETON	K350		25.10.43	24.9.45	NEW WATERFORD	K321	304	21.1.44	22.12.66
CHARLOTTETOWN (II)	K244		28.4.44	7.10.45	ORKNEY	K448		18.4.44	2.9.45
CHEBOGUE	K317		22.2.44	25.9.45	OUTREMONT	K322	310	27.11.43	7.6.65
DUNVER	K 03		11.9.43	2.9.45	PORT COLBORNE	K326		15.11.43	7.11.45
EASTVIEW	K665		3.6.44	11.8.45	PRINCE RUPERT	K324		30.8.43	27.8.45
GROU	K518		5.12.43	27.11.45	ST. CATHARINES	K325	324	31.7.43	31.8.50
JOLIETTE	K418		14.6.44	19.10.45	SAINT JOHN	K456		13.12.43	19.6.45
JONQUIERE	K318	318	10.5.44	16.6.58	SPRINGHILL	K323		21.3.44	2.12.45
KIRKLAND LAKE	K337		21.8.44	4.10.45	STETTLER	K681	311	7.5.44	31.8.65
KOKANEE	K419		6.6.44	19.8.45	STORMONT	K327		27.11.43	9.11.45
LA HULLOISE	K668	305	20.5.44	16.7.65	SWANSEA	K328	306	4.10.43	14.10.66
LONGUEUIL	K672		18.5.44	18.7.45	THETFORD MINES	K459		24.5.44	4.11.45
MAGOG	K673		7.5.44	13.12.44	VALLEYFIELD	K329		7.12.43	7.5.44
MATANE	K444		22.10.43	27.11.45	WASKESIU	K330		16.6.43	22.10.45
MONTREAL	K319		12.11.43	26.7.45	WENTWORTH	K331		7.12.43	10.10.45

RIVER Class,
1943-44 Programme (27)

Particulars same as those of the 1942-43 Programme

	Pendant No.		Commissioned	Paid Off		Pendant No.		Commissioned	Paid Off
ANTIGONISH	K661	301	4.7.44	6.12.66	POUNDMAKER	K675		17.9.44	14.11.45
BUCKINGHAM	K685	314	2.11.44	23.3.65	PRESTONIAN	K662		13.9.44	24.4.56
CAPILANO	K409		25.8.44	26.8.45	ROYALMOUNT	K677		25.8.44	17.11.45
CARLPLACE	K664		13.12.44	2.9.45	RUNNYMEDE	K678		14.6.44	9.8.45
COATICOOK	K410		25.7.44	19.8.45	ST. PIERRE	K680		22.8.44	3.12.45
FORT ERIE	K670	312	27.10.44	26.3.65	ST. STEPHEN	K454	323	28.7.44	31.8.50
GLACE BAY	K414		2.9.44	29.8.45	STE. THERESE	K366	309	28.5.44	6.12.66
HALLOWELL	K666		8.8.44	9.11.45	SEA CLIFF	K344		26.9.44	14.6.45
INCH ARRAN	K667	308	18.11.44	23.6.65	STONE TOWN	K531	302	21.7.44	8.11.45
LANARK	K669	321	6.7.44	19.3.65	STRATHADAM	K682		29.9.44	12.9.45
LASALLE	K519		29.6.44	14.11.45	SUSSEXVALE	K683	313	29.11.44.	6.12.66
LAUZON	K671	322	30.8.44	24.5.63	TORONTO	K538	319	6.5.44	24.4.56
LEVIS (II)	K400		21.7.44	19.9.45	VICTORIAVILLE	K684	320	11.11.44	
PENETANG	K676	316	19.10.44	2.9.55					

RIVER Class,
ex-Royal Navy (7)

Particulars same as those of Canadian-built units

	Pendant No.	Commissioned	Paid Off		Pendant No.	Commissioned	Paid Off
ANNAN	K404	13.6.44	26.5.45	NENE	K270	6.4.44	11.6.45
ETTRICK	K254	29.1.44	28.4.45	RIBBLE	K525	24.7.44	11.6.45
MEON	K269	7.2.44	22.5.45	TEME	K458	28.2.44	3.5.45
MONNOW	K441	8.3.44	11.6.45				

LOCH Class, ex-Royal Navy (3)	1,435	307 x 39 x 14	19.5	c.145	1-4", 6-20 mm. 1 Squid

	Pendant No.	Commissioned	Paid Off
LOCH ACHANALT	K424	31.7.44	20.6.45
LOCH ALVIE	K428	10.8.44	11.6.45
LOCH MORLICH	K517	17.7.44	20.6.45

Minesweepers

BASSET Class (4)	460	163 x 28 x 10	12	3/35	1-4"

	Pendant No.	Commissioned	Paid Off		Pendant No.	Commissioned	Paid Off
COMOX	J64	23.11.38	31.7.45	GASPE	J94	21.10.38	23.7.45
FUNDY	J88	1.9.38	30.7.45	NANOOSE (ex-Nootka)	J35	6.12.38	23.7.45

| BANGOR Class, 1939-40 Programme (18) | 672 | 180 x 29 x 10 | 16 | 6/77 | | 1-4'', 1-2 pdr. 2-20 mm. | | | |

	Pendant No.		Commissioned	Paid Off		Pendant No.		Commissioned	Paid Off
BELLECHASSE	J170		13.12.41	24.8.45	MINAS	J165	189	4.8.41	7.11.55
BURLINGTON	J250		6.9.41	28.10.45	MIRAMICHI	J169		26.11.41	22.10.45
CHEDABUCTO	J168		27.9.41	21.10.43	NIPIGON	J154	188	11.8.41	13.10.45
CHIGNECTO	J160		31.10.41	24.9.45	OUTARDE	J161		4.12.41	4.10.45
CLAYOQUOT	J174		22.8.41	24.12.44	QUATSINO	J152		3.11.41	26.11.45
COWICHAN	J146		4.7.41	7.9.45	QUINTE	J166		30.8.41	3.8.45
GEORGIAN	J144		23.9.41	23.10.45	THUNDER	J156		14.10.41	4.10.45
MAHONE	J159	192	29.9.41	6.11.45	UNGAVA	J149		5.9.41	30.10.45
MALPEQUE	J158	186	4.8.41	9.10.45	WASAGA	J162		1.7.41	6.10.45

BANGOR Class, 1940 Programme, on loan from RN (6) — Particulars same as those of 1939-40 Programme

	Pendant No.	Commissioned	Paid Off		Pendant No.	Commissioned	Paid Off
BAYFIELD	J 08	26.2.42	10.11.45	GUYSBOROUGH	J 52	22.4.42	17.3.45
CANSO	J 21	5.3.42	11.12.45	INGONISH	J 69	8.5.42	2.7.45
CARAQUET	J 38	31.3.42	26.9.45	LOCKEPORT	J100	27.5.42	6.8.45

BANGOR Class, 1940-41 Programme (10) — Particulars same as those of 1939-40 Programme

	Pendant No.		Commissioned	Paid Off		Pendant No.		Commissioned	Paid Off
COURTENAY	J262		21.3.42	2.9.45	KELOWNA	J261		5.2.42	27.10.45
DRUMMONDVILLE	J253	181	30.10.41	29.10.45	MEDICINE HAT	J256	197	4.12.41	6.11.45
GANANOQUE	J259	184	8.11.41	13.10.45	RED DEER	J255	196	24.11.41	30.10.45
GODERICH	J260	198	23.11.41	6.11.45	SWIFT CURRENT	J254	185	11.11.41	23.10.45
GRANDMERE	J258		11.12.41	16.8.45	VEGREVILLE	J257		10.12.41	6.6.45

| BANGOR Class, Diesel, 1940-41 Programme (10) | 590 | 162 x 28 x 9 | 16 | 6/77 | | 1-4'', 1-2 pdrs, 2-20 mm. | | | |

	Pendant No.		Commissioned	Paid Off		Pendant No.		Commissioned	Paid Off
BROCKVILLE	J270	178	19.9.42	3.10.58	MELVILLE	J263		4.12.41	18.8.45
DIGBY	J267	179	26.7.42	14.11.56	NORANDA	J265		15.5.45	28.8.45
ESQUIMALT	J272		26.10.42	16.4.45	TRANSCONA	J271		25.11.42	31.7.45
GRANBY	J264	180	20.6.42	15.12.66	TROIS RIVIERES	J269		12.8.42	31.7.45
LACHINE	J266		2.5.42	10.7.45	TRURO	J268		27.8.42	31.7.45

BANGOR Class, 1941-42 Programme (10) — Particulars same as those of 1939-40 Programme

	Pendant No.		Commissioned	Paid Off		Pendant No.		Commissioned	Paid Off
BLAIRMORE	J314	193	17.11.42	16.10.45	MULGRAVE	J313		4.11.42	25.12.44
FORT WILLIAM	J311	195	25.8.42	23.10.45	PORT HOPE	J280	183	30.7.42	13.10.45
KENORA	J281	191	6.8.42	6.10.45	SARNIA	J309	190	13.8.42	28.10.45
KENTVILLE	J312	182	10.10.42	30.9.54	STRATFORD	J310		29.8.42	13.6.45
MILLTOWN	J317	194	18.9.42	16.10.45	WESTMOUNT	J318	187	15.9.42	13.10.45

ALGERINE Class (12) 990 225 x 36 x 10 16 6/99 1-4", 4-20 mm. Hedgehog

Name	Pendant No.		Commissioned	Paid Off	Name	Pendant No.		Commissioned	Paid Off
BORDER CITIES	J344		18.5.44	5.1.46	PORTAGE	J331	169	22.10.43	26.9.58
FORT FRANCES	J396	170	28.10.44	5.4.46	ROCKCLIFFE	J355	173	30.9.44	15.8.50
KAPUSKASING	J326	171	17.8.44	27.3.46	SAULT STE. MARIE	J334	176	24.6.43	1.10.58
MIDDLESEX	J328		8.6.44	2.12.46	ST. BONIFACE	J332		10.9.43	25.4.47
NEW LISKEARD	J397	169	21.11.44	1.12.69	WALLACEBURG	J336	172	18.11.43	24.9.57
OSHAWA	J330	174	6.7.44	7.11.58	WINNIPEG	J337	177	29.7.43	11.1.46

LLEWELLYN Class (10) 228 119 x 22 x 9 12 2/17 2 machine guns

Name	Pendant No.		Commissioned	Paid Off	Name	Pendant No.		Commissioned	Paid Off
COQUITLAM	J364		25.7.44	3.7.45	LLEWELLYN	J278	141	24.8.42	31.10.51
CRANBROOK	J372		12.5.44	4.11.45	LLOYD GEORGE	J279	142	24.8.42	16.7.48
DAERWOOD	J357		22.4.44	28.11.45	REVELSTOKE	J373		4.7.44	23.10.53
KALAMALKA	J395		2.10.44	19.11.45	ROSSLAND	J358		15.7.44	6.11.45
LAVALLEE	J371		21.6.44	20.8.45	ST. JOSEPH	J359		24.5.44	18.6.45

LAKE Type (10) 360 140 x 28 x 10 10 2 machine guns

Name	Pendant No.	Name	Pendant No.
ALDER LAKE	J480	LARCH LAKE	J489
BEECH LAKE	J482	PINE LAKE	J492
CEDAR LAKE	J484	POPLAR LAKE	J493
ELM LAKE	J486	SPRUCE LAKE	J494
HICKORY LAKE	J488	WILLOW LAKE	J495

BAY Class (20) 412 152 x 28 x 7 16 3/35 1-40 mm.

Name	Pendant No.	Commissioned	Paid Off	Name	Pendant No.	Commissioned	Paid Off
CHALEUR	PFL 144	18.6.54	30.9.54	GASPE (II)	PFL 143	26.11.53	22.8.57
CHALEUR (II)	164	12.9.57		JAMES BAY	152	5.3.54	28.2.64
CHIGNECTO (II)	156	1.12.53	31.3.54	MIRAMICHI (II)	150	30.7.54	1.10.54
CHIGNECTO (III)	160	1.8.57		MIRAMICHI (III)	163	28.10.57	
COMOX (II)	146	2.4.54	11.9.57	QUINTE (II)	149	15.10.54	26.2.64
COWICHAN (II)	147	10.12.53	31.3.54	RESOLUTE	154	16.9.54	14.2.64
COWICHAN (III)	162	12.12.57		THUNDER (II)	153	15.12.53	31.3.54
FORTUNE	151	3.11.54	28.2.64	THUNDER (III)	161	3.10.57	
FUNDY (II)	145	19.3.54	31.3.54	TRINITY	157	16.6.54	21.8.57
FUNDY (III)	159	27.11.56		UNGAVA (II)	148	4.6.54	23.8.57

Anti-Submarine Trawlers

WESTERN ISLES Class (8)   530   164 x 28 x 9   12   4/36   1-12 pdr., 1-20 mm.

	Pendant No.	Commissioned	Paid Off		Pendant No.	Commissioned	Paid Off
ANTICOSTI	T274	8.8.42	17.6.45	LISCOMB	T285	3.9.42	17.6.45
BAFFIN	T275	20.8.42	1.9.45	MAGDALEN	T279	19.8.42	17.6.45
CAILIFF	T276	17.9.42	11.7.45	MANITOULIN	T280	8.9.42	17.6.45
IRONBOUND	T284	5.10.42	17.6.45	MISCOU	T277	20.10.42	17.6.45

Armed Yachts

	Displacement (tons)	Dimensions (feet)	Top Speed (knots)	Crew	Commissioned	Paid Off	Armament	Remarks
AMBLER (ex-*Cynthia*)	273	130 x 23 x 10	9	4/17	6.5.40	20.7.45		Built 1922
BEAVER (ex-*Aztec*)	808	260 x 28 x 13	12	5/45	30.9.40	17.10.44	1-4"	Built 1902
CARIBOU (ex-*Elfreda*)	306	142 x 23 x 9	11	5/35	27.5.40	20.7.45	1-12 pdr.	Built 1928
COUGAR (ex-*Breezin' Thru*)	204	140 x 20 x 10	10	5/35	11.9.40	23.11.45	1-6 pdr.	Built 1916
ELK (ex-*Arcadia*)	578	188 x 27 x 11	11	5/35	10.9.40	4.8.45	1-4"	Built 1926
GRIZZLY (ex-*Machigonne*)	195	140 x 19 x 10	12	5/35	17.7.41	17.6.44	1-6 pdr.	Built 1909
HUSKY (ex-*Wild Duck*)	360	153 x 25 x 10	10	5/35	23.7.40	3.8.45	1-4"	Built 1930
LYNX (ex-*Ramona*)	495	181 x 24 x 9	10	5/35	26.8.40	23.4.42	1-4"	Built 1922
MOOSE (ex-*Cleopatra*)	263	130 x 22 x 9	12	5/35	8.9.40	20.7.45	1-12 pdr.	Built 1930
OTTER (ex-*Conseco*)	419	160 x 25 x 10	10	5/35	4.10.40	26.3.41	1-4"	Built 1921
RACCOON (ex-*Halonia*)	377	148 x 25 x 10	11	5/35	17.5.40	7.9.42	1-12 pdr.	Built 1931
REINDEER (ex-*Mascotte*)	337	140 x 24 x 9	11	5/35	25.7.40	20.7.45	1-4"	Built 1926
RENARD (ex-*Winchester*)	411	225 x 21 x 8	15	5/35	27.5.40	1.8.44	1-12 pdr., 2-TT	Built 1916
SANS PEUR (ex-*Trenora*)	856	210 x 30 x 13	13	5/43	12.10.39	31.1.47	1-4", 1-2 pdr.	Built 1933
VISON (ex-*Avalon*)	422	181 x 24 x 13	10	5/35	5.10.40	4.8.45	1-12 pdr.	Built 1931
WOLF (ex-*Blue Water*)	320	172 x 23 x 10	10	5/38	2.10.40	16.5.45	1-12 pdr., 1-2 pdr.	Built 1915

Submarines		Displacement (tons)	Dimensions (feet)	Top Speed (knots)	Crew	Commissioned	Paid Off	Armament
CC 1 (ex-*Iquique*)		313/421	144 x 15 x 11	13/10	2/16	6.8.14	12.12.18	5-18" TT
CC 2 (ex-*Antofagasta*)		313/421	152 x 15 x 11	13/10	2/16	6.8.14	12.12.18	3-18" TT
CH 14 and CH 15 (ex-H14 and 15)		364/434	150 x 16 x 12	13/11	4/18	6.19	30.6.22	4-18" TT
U 190 and U 889		1,120/1,232	252 x 22 x 15	18/7		14.5.45	24.7.47 (U 190) 12.1.46 (U 889)	6-21" TT 2-37 mm. (1 x II) 4-20 mm. (2 x II)
GRILSE (ex- USS *Burrfish*)	SS71	1,525/2,415	312 x 27 x 17	20/10	8/74	11.5.61	2.10.69	10-21" TT
RAINBOW (II) (ex-USS *Argonaut*)	SS75	1,570/2,415	312 x 27 x 17	20/10	8/74	2.12.68	31.12.74	10-21" TT
"O" Class (3)		2,030/2,410	295 x 26 x 18	12/17	7/58			8-21" TT

	Pendant No.	Commissioned	Paid Off
OJIBWA	SS 72	23.9.65	
OKANAGAN	SS 74	22.6.68	
ONONDAGA	SS 73	22.6.67	

Motor Craft

		Displacement (tons)	Dimensions (feet)	Top Speed (knots)	Crew	Commissioned	Paid Off	Armament
Motor Torpedo Boats (11) MTB 459 to 466, 485, 486 and 491 (British Power Boat 'G' Type)		41	72 x 21 x 5	43	3/14			1-2 pdr., 2-20 mm. (1 x II) 2-18" TT
Motor Torpedo Boats (10) MTB 726, 727, 735, 736 743 to 746, 748 and 797 (Fairmile 'D' Type)		102	115 x 21 x 5	30	4/28			2-6 pdr., 2-20 mm. (1 x II) 4-.5" m.g. (2 x II) 4-18" TT
Motor Launches (80) ML 050 to 129 (Fairmile 'B' Type)		79	112 x 18 x 5	20	3/14			3-20 mm.

Arctic Patrol Vessel

		Displacement (tons)	Dimensions (feet)	Top Speed (knots)	Crew	Commissioned	Paid Off	Armament
LABRADOR	AW 50	6,490 full load	269 x 63 x 29	16	224	8.7.54	19.11.57	2-40 mm.

Operational Support Ships (3)

		Displacement (tons)	Dimensions (feet)	Top Speed (knots)	Crew	Commissioned	Paid Off	Armament
PROVIDER	AOR 508	22,700 full load	551 x 76 x 30	20	169	28.9.63		
PRESERVER	AOR 510	24,000 full load	555 x 76 x 30	20	227	30.7.70		2-3" (1 x II)
PROTECTEUR	AOR 509	24,000 full load	555 x 76 x 30	20	227	30.8.69		2-3" (1 x II)

Pendant Numbers, Wartime

G	07	Athabaskan (I)	J100	Lockeport	J280	Port Hope	K	03	Dunver
	24	Huron	144	Georgian	281	Kenora		15	Atholl
	63	Haida	146	Cowichan	309	Sarnia		101	Nanaimo
	89	Iroquois	148	Malpeque	310	Stratford		103	Alberni
			149	Ungava	311	Fort William		104	Dawson
H	00	Restigouche	152	Quatsino	312	Kentville		106	Edmunston
	31	Ottawa (II)	154	Nipigon	313	Mulgrave		110	Shediac
	48	Fraser	156	Thunder	314	Blairmore		112	Matapedia
	49	Margaree	159	Mahone	317	Milltown		113	Arvida
	60	Ottawa (I)	160	Chignecto	318	Westmount		115	Lévis (I)
	61	Gatineau	161	Outarde	326	Kapuskasing		116	Chambly
	69	Qu'Appelle	162	Wasaga	328	Middlesex		118	Napanee
	70	Saskatchewan	165	Minas	330	Oshawa		119	Orillia
	75	Kootenay	166	Quinte	331	Portage		121	Rimouski
	83	St. Laurent	168	Chedabucto	332	St. Boniface		124	Cobalt
	96	Buxton	169	Miramichi	334	Sault Ste. Marie		125	Kenogami
	99	Chaudière	170	Bellechasse	336	Wallaceburg		127	Algoma
			174	Clayoquot	337	Winnipeg		129	Agassiz
I	04	Annapolis	250	Burlington	344	Border Cities		131	Chilliwack
	18	Assiniboine	253	Drummondville	355	Rockcliffe		133	Quesnel
	24	Hamilton	254	Swift Current	357	Daerwood		136	Shawinigan
	49	Columbia	255	Red Deer	358	Rossland		138	Barrie
	57	Niagara	256	Medicine Hat	359	St. Joseph		139	Moncton
	59	Skeena	257	Vegreville	364	Coquitlam		141	Summerside
	65	St. Clair	258	Grandmère	371	Lavallée		143	Louisburg (I)
	79	Saguenay	259	Gananoque	372	Cranbrook		145	Arrowhead
	81	St. Croix	260	Goderich	373	Revelstoke		146	Pictou
	93	St. Francis	261	Kelowna	395	Kalamalka		147	Baddeck
			262	Courtenay	396	Fort Frances		148	Amherst
J	08	Bayfield	263	Melville	397	New Liskeard		149	Brandon
	21	Canso	264	Granby	480	Alder Lake		150	Eyebright
	29	Armentières	265	Noranda	482	Beech Lake		151	Lunenburg
	35	Nanoose	266	Lachine	484	Cedar Lake		152	Sherbrooke
	38	Caraquet	267	Digby	486	Elm Lake		160	Lethbridge
	46	Festubert	268	Truro	488	Hickory Lake		161	Prescott
	52	Guysborough	269	Trois Rivières	489	Larch Lake		162	Sudbury
	64	Comox	270	Brockville	492	Pine Lake		163	Galt
	69	Ingonish	271	Transcona	493	Poplar Lake		164	Moose Jaw
	70	Ypres	272	Esquimalt	494	Spruce Lake		165	Battleford
	88	Fundy	278	Llewellyn	495	Willow Lake		166	Snowberry
	94	Gaspé	279	Lloyd George				153	Sorel

K154 Camrose	K273 La Malbaie	K414 Glace Bay	K665 Eastview
155 Windflower	317 Chebogue	415 Hawkesbury	666 Hallowell
156 Chicoutimi	318 Jonquière	418 Joliette	667 Inch Arran
157 Dauphin	319 Montreal	419 Kokanee	668 La Hulloise
158 Saskatoon	320 New Glasgow	424 Loch Achanalt	669 Lanark
159 Hepatica	321 New Waterford	428 Loch Alvie	670 Fort Erie
167 Drumheller	322 Outremont	440 Lachute	671 Lauzon
168 The Pas	323 Springhill	441 Monnow	672 Longueuil
169 Rosthern	324 Prince Rupert	444 Matane	673 Magog
170 Morden	325 St. Catharines	448 Orkney	675 Poundmaker
171 Kamsack	326 Port Colborne	454 St. Stephen	676 Penetang
172 Trillium	327 Stormont	455 Strathroy	677 Royalmount
173 Weyburn	328 Swansea	456 Saint John	678 Runnymede
174 Trail	329 Valleyfield	457 Stellarton	680 St. Pierre
175 Wetaskiwin	330 Waskesiu	458 Teme	681 Stettler
176 Kamloops	331 Wentworth	459 Thetford Mines	682 Strathadam
177 Dunvegan	332 Belleville	485 Mimico	683 Sussexvale
178 Oakville	333 Cobourg	486 Forest Hill	684 Victoriaville
179 Buctouche	335 Frontenac	487 Long Branch	685 Buckingham
180 Collingwood	337 Kirkland Lake	488 St. Thomas	686 Fergus
181 Sackville	338 Lindsay	489 Hespeler	687 Guelph
182 Bittersweet	339 North Bay	490 Kincardine	688 Merrittonia
191 Mayflower	340 Owen Sound	491 Orangeville	
194 Fennel	341 Parry Sound	492 Leaside	R 04 Cayuga
198 Spikenard	342 Peterborough	493 Bowmanville	10 Micmac
218 Brantford	343 St. Lambert	494 Arnprior	16 Crescent
220 Midland	344 Sea Cliff	495 Copper Cliff	17 Algonquin
223 Timmins	345 Smiths Falls	496 Tillsonburg	20 Crusader
225 Kitchener	346 Whitby	497 Humberstone	64 Sioux
228 New Westminster	350 Cape Breton	498 Petrolia	79 Athabaskan (II)
229 Dundas	357 Rivière du Loup	499 Huntsville	89 Iroquois
231 Calgary	358 Asbestos	517 Loch Morlich	96 Nootka
233 Port Arthur	366 Ste. Thérèse	518 Grou	
234 Regina	368 Trentonian	519 Lasalle	T274 Anticosti
237 Halifax	369 West York	520 Norsyd	275 Baffin
238 Woodstock	394 Thorlock	525 Ribble	276 Cailiff
240 Vancouver	400 Lévis (II)	531 Stonetown	277 Miscou
242 Ville de Québec	401 Louisburg (II)	538 Toronto	279 Magdalen
244 Charlottetown (I & II)	402 Giffard	540 Beauharnois	280 Manitoulin
245 Fredericton	404 Annan	661 Antigonish	284 Ironbound
254 Ettrick	407 Beacon Hill	662 Prestonian	285 Liscomb
269 Meon	409 Capilano	663 Cap de la Madeleine	
270 Nene	410 Coaticook	664 Carlplace	

Pendant Numbers, 1949 onward

141	Llewellyn	188	Nipigon	280	Iroquois (II)
142	Lloyd George	189	Minas	281	Huron (II)
143	Gaspé (II)	190	Sarnia	282	Athabaskan (III)
144	Chaleur (I)	191	Kenora	283	Algonquin (II)
145	Fundy (II)	192	Mahone	301	Antigonish
146	Comox (II)	193	Blairmore	302	Stonetown
147	Cowichan (II)	194	Milltown	303	Beacon Hill
148	Ungava (II)	195	Fort William	304	New Waterford
149	Quinte (II)	196	Red Deer	305	La Hulloise
150	Miramichi (II)	197	Medicine Hat	306	Swansea
151	Fortune	198	Goderich	307	Prestonian
152	James Bay	205	St. Laurent (II)	308	Inch Arran
153	Thunder (II)	206	Saguenay (II)	309	Ste. Thérèse
154	Resolute	207	Skeena (II)	310	Outremont
156	Chignecto (II)	213	Nootka	311	Stettler
157	Trinity	214	Micmac	312	Fort Erie
158	Cordova	215	Haida	313	Sussexvale
159	Fundy (III)	216	Huron (I)	314	Buckingham
160	Chignecto (III)	217	Iroquois (I)	315	New Glasgow
161	Thunder (III)	218	Cayuga	316	Penetang
162	Cowichan (III)	219	Athabaskan (II)	317	Cap de la Madeleine
163	Miramichi (III)	224	Algonquin (I)	318	Jonquière
164	Chaleur (II)	225	Sioux	319	Toronto
168	New Liskeard	226	Crescent	320	Victoriaville
169	Portage	228	Crusader	321	Lanark
170	Fort Frances	229	Ottawa (III)	322	Lauzon
171	Kapuskasing	230	Margaree (II)	323	St. Stephen
172	Wallaceburg	233	Fraser (II)	324	St. Catharines
173	Rockcliffe	234	Assiniboine (II)	400	Bras d'Or
174	Oshawa	235	Chaudière (II)	508	Provider
176	Sault Ste. Marie	236	Gatineau (II)	509	Protecteur
177	Winnipeg	256	St. Croix (II)	510	Preserver
178	Brockville	257	Restigouche (II)		
179	Digby	258	Kootenay (II)		
180	Granby	259	Terra Nova		
181	Drummondville	260	Columbia (II)		
182	Kentville	261	Mackenzie		
183	Port Hope	262	Saskatchewan (II)		
184	Gananoque	263	Yukon		
185	Swift Current	264	Qu'Appelle (II)		
186	Malpeque	265	Annapolis (II)		
187	Westmount	266	Nipigon (II)		

INDEX OF SHIPS OF THE R.C.N.

Agassiz, 54, 102
Alberni, 54, 102
Alder Lake, 107
Algoma, 102
Algonquin (I), 41, 42, **46,** 101
Algonquin (II), 69, 102
Ambler, 62, 108
Amherst, 102
Annan, 105
Annapolis (I), 33, 100
Annapolis (II), 66, 102
Anticosti, **55,** 108
Antigonish, 60, 105
Arnprior, 104
Arrowhead, 54, 102
Arvida, 102
Asbestos, 104
Assiniboine (I), 26, 28, 31, 100
Assiniboine (II), 101
Athabaskan (I), 35, **35,** 36, 100
Athabaskan (II), 42, **43,** 100
Athabaskan (III), 102
Atholl, 103
Aurora, 9, **9,** 99

Baddeck, 102
Baffin, 108
Barrie, **51,** 102
Battleford, 102
Bayfield, 106
Beacon Hill, 60, 104
Beauharnois, 104
Beaver (I), 108
Beaver (II), 91
Beech Lake, 107
Bellechasse, 106
Belleville, 104
Bittersweet, 102
Blairmore, 106

Bonaventure, 22, **22,** 23, **23,** 70, 99
Border Cities, 107
Bowmanville, 104
Brandon, **53,** 102
Brantford, 103
Bras d'Or, 70, **71,** 102
Brockville, 72, 106
Buckingham, 60, 105
Buctouche, 102
Burlington, 106
Buxton, 33, 100

CC 1, 80, **81,** 109
CC 2, 80, **81,** 109
CH 14, 80, **82,** 109
CH 15, 80, **82,** 109
Cailiff, 108
Calgary, 103
Camrose, 102
Canso, 106
Cap de la Madeleine, 60, 104
Cape Breton, 104
Capilano, 105
Caribou, 108
Caraquet, 106
Carlplace, 105
Cayuga, 42, 100
Cedar Lake, 107
Chaleur (I), 107
Chaleur (II), 107
Chambly, 52, 102
Champlain, 24, **26,** 99
Charlottetown (I), 54, 103
Charlottetown (II), 104
Charybdis, 3, **4**
Chaudière (I), 39, 40, 100
Chaudière (II), **65,** 101
Chebogue, 59, 104

Chedabucto, 78, 106
Chicoutimi, 102
Chignecto (I), 106
Chignecto (II), 107
Chignecto (III), 107
Chilliwack, 52, 102
Clayoquot, **74,** 78, 106
Coaticook, 105
Cobalt, 102
Cobourg, **50,** 103
Collingwood, 102
Columbia (I), 33, 100
Columbia (II), 101
Comox (I), 72, 105
Comox (II), 107
Copper Cliff, 104
Coquitlam, 107
Cougar (I), 108
Cougar (II), 91
Courtenay, 106
Cowichan (I), 106
Cowichan (II), 107
Cowichan (III), 107
Cranbrook, 107
Crescent, 44, 46, 101
Crusader, 44, **45,** 46, **47,** 101

Daerwood, 107
Dauphin, 102
Dawson, 52, 102
Digby, 72, 106
Drumheller, 102
Drummondville, 106
Dundas, 52, 103
Dunvegan, 102
Dunver, 104

Eastview, 104
Edmunston, 52, 102

Elk (I), 108
Elk (II), 91
Elm Lake, 107
Esquimalt, **75,** 78, 106
Ettrick, 105
Eyebright, 102

Fennel, 102
Fergus, 103
Forest Hill, 104
Fort Erie, 60, 105
Fort Frances, 107
Fort William, 106
Fortune, 107
Fraser (I), 24, **27,** 28, 100
Fraser (II), 101
Fredericton, 52, 103
Frontenac, 103
Fundy (I), 72, 105
Fundy (II), 107
Fundy (III), 107

Galt, 102
Gananoque, 106
Gaspé (I), 72, 105
Gaspé (II), 107
Gatineau (I), 39, 100
Gatineau (II), 101
Georgian, 106
Giffard, 104
Glace Bay, 105
Goderich, 106
Granby, 60, 72, 106
Grandmère, 106
Grilse, 84, **85,** 109
Grizzly, 108
Grou, 104
Guelph, 103
Guysborough, 78, 106

Haida, 35, 36, 37, 42, **44,** 100

Halifax, 52, 103
Hallowell, 105
Hamilton, 33, 100
Hawkesbury, 103
Hepatica, 54, 102
Hespeler, 104
Hickory Lake, 107
Humberstone, 104
Huntsville, 104
Huron (I), 35, 36, **37,** 42, 100
Huron (II), 102
Husky, 108

Inch Arran, 60, 105
Ingonish, 106
Ironbound, 108
Iroquois (I), 35, 36, 37, 42, 100
Iroquois (II), **69,** 102

James Bay, 107
Joliette, **59,** 104
Jonquière, 60, 104

Kalamalka, 107
Kamloops, 102
Kamsack, 102
Kapuskasing, **76,** 107
Kelowna, 106
Kenogami, 102
Kenora, 106
Kentville, 72, 106
Kincardine, 104
Kirkland Lake, 104
Kitchener, 103
Kokanee, 104
Kootenay (I), 39, **40,** 100
Kootenay (II), 101

La Hulloise, **57,** 60, 104
La Malbaie, 103
Labrador, 92, **93,** 109

Lachine, 106
Lachute, 104
Lanark, 60, 105
Larch Lake, 107
Lasalle, 105
Lauzon, 60, 105
Lavallée, 107
Leaside, **55,** 104
Lethbridge, 52, 102
Lévis (I), 54, 102
Lévis (II), 105
Lindsay, 103
Liscomb, 108
Llewellyn, **77,** 107
Lloyd George, 107
Loch Achanalt, 105
Loch Alvie, **58,** 105
Loch Morlich, 105
Lockeport, 106
Long Branch, 104
Longueuil, 104
Louisburg (I), 54, 102
Louisburg (II), 103
Lunenburg, 102
Lynx, 108

ML 121, **91**
MTB 459, **89**
MTB 745, **90**
Mackenzie, 64,**68,** 101
Magdalen, 108
Magnificent, **21,** 22, 99
Magog, 59, 104
Mahone, 106
Malpeque, 106
Manitoulin, 108
Margaree (I), 28, 100
Margaree (II), 101
Matane, 104
Matapedia, 102
Mayflower, 102

Medicine Hat, 106
Melville, 106
Meon, 105
Merrittonia, 104
Micmac, **37,** 42, 100
Middlesex, 76, 107
Midland, 103
Mimico, 104
Minas, 72, 106
Milltown, 106
Miramichi (I), 106
Miramichi (II), 107
Miramichi (III), 107
Miscou, 108
Moncton, 102
Monnow, 105
Montreal, 104
Moose (I), 108
Moose (II), 91
Moose Jaw, 52, 102
Morden, 102
Mulgrave, 106

Nabob, 16, **17,** 99
Nanaimo, 102
Nanoose, 72, 105
Napanee, 102
Nene, 105
New Glasgow, 60, **61,** 104
New Liskeard, 107
New Waterford, 60, 104
New Westminster, 52, 103
Niagara, 33, **34,** 100
Niobe, 5, **7, 8,** 99
Nipigon (I), 106
Nipigon (II), 66, **67,** 102
Nootka (I), 72, **73**
Nootka (II), 42, 100
Noranda, 106
Norsyd, 103
North Bay, 103

Oakville, 52, 102
Ojibwa, 84, **86,** 109
Okanagan, 84, 109
Onondaga, 84, 109
Ontario, **10,** 11, 99
Orangeville, 104
Orillia, 102
Orkney, 104
Oshawa, 107
Ottawa (I), 24, 32, 100
Ottawa (II), 39, 40, 100
Ottawa (III), 101
Otter, 62, 108
Outarde, 106
Outremont, 60, 104
Owen Sound, 103'

Parry Sound, 104
Patrician, 24, 99
Patriot, 24, **25,** 99
Penetang, 60, **60,** 105
Peterborough, 104
Petrolia, 104
Pictou, 102
Pine Lake, **78,** 107
Poplar Lake, 107
Port Arthur, 103
Port Colborne, 104
Port Hope, 106
Portage, 76, 107
Poundmaker, 105
Prescott, 102
Preserver, 94, 109
Prestonian, 60, 105
Prince David, 12, 14, 15, 99
Prince Henry, 12, 14, **15,** 99
Prince Robert, 12, **13, 14,**
   15, 99
Prince Rupert, 104
Protecteur, 94, **96,** 109
Provider, 94, **95,** 109

Puncher, 16, **18, 19,** 99

Qu'Appelle (I), 39, 100
Qu'Appelle (II), 101
Quatsino, 106
Quebec, 11, **11,** 99
Quesnel, 52, 102
Quinte (I), 106
Quinte (II), 107

Raccoon (I), 62, 108
Raccoon (II), 91
Rainbow (I), 5, **6,** 99
Rainbow (II), 84, **86,** 109
Red Deer, 106
Regina, 54, 103
Reindeer (I), 108
Reindeer (II), 91
Renard, 108
Resolute, **79,** 107
Restigouche (I), 24, 28, **31,** 100
Restigouche (II), 101
Revelstoke, 107
Ribble, 105
Rimouski, 103
Rivière du Loup, 103
Rockcliffe, 107
Rossland, 107
Rosthern, 103
Royalmount, 105
Runnymede, 105

Sackville, 54, 103
Saguenay (I), 24, 28, **29,** 99
Saguenay (II), 101
St. Boniface, 107
St. Catharines, **59,** 104
St. Clair, 33, 100
St. Croix (I), **32,** 33, 100
St. Croix (II), 101
St. Francis, 33, 100

Saint John, 56, 104
St. Joseph, 107
St. Lambert, 103
St. Laurent (I), 24, 28, **30, 37,** 100
St. Laurent (II), 64, **66,** 101
St. Pierre, 105
St. Stephen, 105
St. Thomas, 104
Ste. Thérèse, 60, 105
Sans Peur, 62, 108
Sarnia, 106
Saskatchewan (I), **37, 38,** 39, 100
Saskatchewan (II), 101
Saskatoon, 103
Sault Ste. Marie, 76, 107
Sea Cliff, 105
Shawinigan, 54, 103
Shediac, 33, 103
Sherbrooke, 103
Sioux, **37, 41,** 42, 101
Skeena (I), 24, 28, **30,** 31, 99
Skeena (II), 101
Smiths Falls, 104
Snowberry, 52, 103
Sorel, 103
Spikenard, 54, 103
Springhill, 104
Spruce Lake, 107
Stellarton, 104
Stettler, 60, 104

Stonetown, 105
Stormont, 60, 104
Stratford, 106
Strathadam, 105
Strathroy, 104
Sudbury, 52, 103
Summerside, 103
Sussexvale, 60, 105
Swansea, 56, 59, 60, 104
Swift Current, 106

Teme, 59, 105
Terra Nova, 64, 101
The Pas, 52, 103
Thetford Mines, **59,** 104
Thorlock, 104
Thunder (I), 106
Thunder (II), 107
Thunder (III), 107
Tillsonburg, 104
Timmins, 52, 103
Toronto, 60, 105
Trail, 103
Transcona, 106
Trentonian, 54, 103
Trillium, 103
Trinity, 107
Trois Rivières, 106
Truro, 106

U 190, **59,** 82, 109
U 889, **59,** 82, **83, 91,** 109

Uganda, 10, 11, **11,** 99
Ungava (I), 106
Ungava (II), 107

Valleyfield, 59, 104
Vancouver (I), 24, 99
Vancouver (II), 52, 103
Vegreville, 106
Victoriaville, 60, 105
Ville de Québec, 103
Vison, **63,** 108

Wallaceburg, 76, 107
Warrior, 20, **20,** 99
Wasaga, 106
Waskesiu, 104
Wentworth, 104
West York, 104
Westmount, 106
Wetaskiwin, **49,** 103
Weyburn, 54, 103
Whitby, 103
Willow Lake, 107
Windflower, 54, 103
Winnipeg, 107
Wolf (I), 108
Wolf (II), 91
Woodstock, 54, 103

Yukon, 64, 101